Fifties Furniture

Leslie Piña

Schiffer Publishing Ltd

77 Lower Valley Road, Atglen, PA 19310

for the students in my 20th-Century Furniture class

Library of Congress Cataloging-in-Publication Data

Piña, Leslie A., 1947-
  Fifties furniture / Leslie Piña
    p. cm.
  Includes bibliographical references and index.
  ISBN 0-7643-0152-7 (hardcover)
  1. Furniture--History--20th century. 2. Decoration and ornament--
International style. I. Title.
NK2397.P56 1996
749.20495--dc20   96-22060
                                                   CIP

ISBN: 0-7643-0152-7

Published by Schiffer Publishing, Ltd.
77 Lower Valley Road
Atglen, PA 19310
Phone: (610) 593-1777
Please write for a free catalog.
This book may be purchased from the publisher.
Please include $2.95 for shipping.
Try your bookstore first.

We are interested in hearing from authors with
book ideas on related subjects.

Credits

Direct contact with objects is obviously the best way to learn about them. Museums provide one kind of direct experience, and ideally, the museum exhibit serves as a model by which to gauge quality and significance. At museums, however, contact is almost always limited to the visual and intellectual. This is understandable because objects in permanent displays would quickly become worn and damaged if the public were permitted to handle them. The place to handle and examine decorative arts is where a steady turnover is assumed, and that is the marketplace. With the museum on hand as a reference, the antique shop, mall, or show, and the auction preview take on an added role of classroom; the illustrated auction catalog serves as textbook for teaching attribution, market trends, and relative value.

I have often devoted more time studying auction catalogs than books on similar subjects. That is not to say that there are not many wonderful books available — there are. But the auction catalog is the next best thing to coming into physical contact with hundreds of different objects each time the pages are turned, and I would like to acknowledge the auction houses, especially the two major international leaders, Sotheby's and Christie's, for the contribution they have been making to scholarship and to collecting in general. In addition, I wish to again thank both Sotheby's and Christie's for generously lending photographs of objects from their beautiful auction catalogs.

There are also other fine auction houses that publish illustrated catalogs, and I wish to thank two in particular whose contribution to modern decorative arts has been exemplary. Don Treadway Gallery and Associates of Cincinnati, Ohio has been holding regular twentieth century auctions in Chicago. Skinner, Inc. Auctioneers and Appraisers of Antiques and Fine Art, Boston and Bolton, Massachusetts has held regular auctions of twentieth century design in addition to other regular sales in a wide range of specialties. My thanks to these two companies for so graciously loaning photographs from their excellent catalogs (a list of specific sales is in the bibliography).

A special thanks is due to another source for photographs, information, and inspiration. The international furniture companies that originally produced most of the modern classics, Herman Miller, and Knoll, kindly lent photographs of many of these design gems. Though not aimed at the residential market, Steelcase and Stow Davis also contributed to modernism and to this book by lending photographs of offices. Thanks to William Blitzer of Lightolier, Phil Miller of Howard Miller Clock, Bruce Hinrichs of Stow Davis, and Linda Folland and Robert Viol at Herman Miller. I also wish to thank Herman Miller, Knoll, and Steelcase for the hospitality they extended to my students when we visited Grand Rapids, and for allowing me to photograph their displays.

Ramón and I took the remainder of the pictures, usually under less-than-ideal conditions. Thanks to the Cuyahoga County Public Library Beachwood Branch, and to Studio Moderne, and Suite Lorain Antiques, both in Cleveland, Ohio, for allowing us to disrupt their environments with lights and tripods. Again, I would like to acknowledge the invaluable service provided by libraries, with special thanks to the Ursuline College library and Ralph and Terry Kovel who have been most generous with the use of their library. Paula Ockner has again taken on the responsibility of proofreading, and again, any remaining errors are mine. Nancy and Peter Schiffer have been admirably patient, but I am glad that they finally said, "Let's get this book to press already." Thanks to Jeff Snyder and the whole crew at Schiffer's for the part each one plays in the book building process.

Contents

Perhaps the phrase "circa Fifties Furniture" would more accurately reflect the meaning of this book's title. "Circa," around or about, usually refers to a date, so "circa fifties" should mean "around the 1950s," and it does. "Around" can mean a few years before or after the 1950s or a decade or more, depending on the context. However, "Fifties" has come to denote more than a set of years; it has come to mean a particular look or style that is associated with those years. Like any style, there is a range of variations or sub-styles and, in the case of Fifties, the element that holds these together is modernism. Whether Fifties furniture, textile design, or an accessory such as a clock or lamp, the intent of the designer and of the contemporary consumer, or user, of the items was to explore new expressions of modernism.

At least five styles preceded and influenced Fifties modern: (1) Art Moderne (later included in the catch-all term, Art Deco), the French elitist handicraft style that peaked at the 1925 Paris International Exposition, which in its American translation is usually associated with the years between the wars; (2) Bauhaus and the International Style, the German school and style of about the same years as Art Moderne but intended for mass production, and is there-fore slick, of new materials, and devoid of ornament to the point of austerity; (3) Machine Age Modern, an intentionally democratic and popular American style also associated with industrial design and mass production in the 1930s and 1940s, which got its stylistic cues — aerodynamic curves and geometric simplicity — from both Art Moderne and Bauhaus; (4) Biomorphism, a very specific organic curvilinear look using surreal amoeboid forms derived from the fine arts; and (5) Abstract Expressionism, another contribution from painting which encouraged designers to further expand and explore nonrepresentational themes.

All of these styles were modern in the sense of consciously breaking or attempting to break from tradition and the past. When expressed in Fifties style, they may be found in combination with one another or as an apparent reconciliation between two extremes. For example, Bauhaus and Machine Age Modern, although both tied to industrial design, represent opposing views: Bauhaus avoidance of ornament versus Machine Age reliance on ornament reduced to cliche; Bauhaus rationalism and idealism versus Machine Age theatricality and glitz. This stylistic hunger for popularity led to a sixth element, one necessarily from the period of the 1950s, which also helped to define the style — popular culture. Less-than-serious themes and motifs, from French poodles to American cowboys, were used for inexpensive items that rode along for the modern ride. Today, these may evoke labels like "camp" or "kitsch," but they are difficult to ignore. When it comes to Fifties, there is a fine line between the so-called high style and the more tongue-in-cheek versions.

Circa Fifties, then, means around or about that style or collection of styles referred to as Fifties and of the years more loosely called mid-century. Understandably, there is considerable latitude in selecting objects for a book with such a title. What follows in these pages then is a combination of mostly high style designer Fifties modern, some popular Fifties modern, plus examples from both categories that were produced a bit beyond the time boundaries of the 1950s. Now with such a potentially unwieldy definition, the objects selected to represent such a theme require additional criteria if the results are to be at all manageable, so I have sampled two rather specific, yet compatible collecting categories. The first category, which might be called "classics," includes well-known and well-liked designs, some of which have become so popular that they have been recently reissued, or at least re-emphasized, by their makers. These include several Herman Miller and Knoll furniture classics, and some Heywood-Wakefield designs. The other category includes a growing list of designers and companies that are known to a group of specialist collectors and dealers but are not yet household names. Proto-classics? Some of the Scandinavian Modern furniture, accessories such as lighting, or tile plaques by Harris Strong fall into this category.

Naturally, the list of names and objects selected for this book is somewhat tentative and open to revision or discussion — perhaps soon. I am not presuming to form a definition but to provide a visual sample of a phenomenon that is already happening. Fifties is too recent to be called "antique," yet it is already being treated as such. Collecting and scholarship are dynamic, particularly when collectors and researchers have lived through or lived with things from the period. Movement and change, discovery and rediscovery, are elements that keep authors writing and make the decorative arts fields lively, and circa Fifties promises to be among the liveliest.

Value Guide

Furniture is different from glassware or pottery with regard to pricing. Condition will vary from the rare perfect piece to those showing degrees of wear and use. Furniture was used in someone's home, some pieces more lovingly than others. Prices will be affected by variations of condition and recondition or restoration. In addition, each region of the country will have a market directed by supply and demand, by individual tastes, and by fashions or trends. In the case of circa Fifties furniture, the major coastal cities will have the largest and most established markets, and perhaps the highest prices. Auctions help to guide or set prices as well, but auctions are events, and once the lots are sold, similar examples at future sales may bring very different prices. In addition, companies such as Herman Miller and Knoll, which have continu-ously produced or have reissued designs, have standardized listed prices that are probably higher, though sometimes lower, than the "antique" or vintage examples.

With this in mind, it is clear that any price guide for this particular category of collectible decorative art is apt to be uneven, to say the least, and neither the author nor the publisher can be responsible for any outcomes from consulting such a guide. Our intent is to give a general idea of some typical prices that similar items have recently sold for and might sell for again. Prices are in United States dollars and are listed in the order of the object in the caption, except for some vintage photos, such as offices. Current list prices for new items can be found by contacting the companies in the resource list.

Diamond chair designed by Harry Bertoia for Knoll, chromed frame, upholstered in beige hopsack with seam at midpoint. *Photo courtesy Christie's New York.*

Designers and Makers

Before there was mass production or mass consumption, before there were materials such as plastics, before there were techniques for molding fiberglass, bending plywood, or tubing metal, furniture was made by hand of solid wood. Designers and makers of circa fifties furniture have had a different kind of relationship from designers and makers of the past, where in many instances they were one and the same. Evidence suggests that attributes such as comfort, accessibility, and affordability were regarded little, if at all, by furniture makers in the remote past. European craftsmen and their clients were usually more interested in the aesthetics of ornament and in the technical feats performed in producing it. An elite clientele could afford to pay for the time and the skills invested in hand carving a ball and claw foot on a cabriolet leg from a single block of wood or the carving, inlay, or gilding of elaborate surface decorations. As long as these wealthy patrons supported this labor intensive handicraft, its designers and craftsmen continued to provide ornamental furniture for centuries.

Ordinary people in Europe and Colonial America, if they owned any furniture, probably built it themselves or had it made locally by a builder or a joiner. Practicality, function, and low cost were necessarily top priorities. Design of common furniture was therefore straightforward, and neither comfort nor aesthetics were given much attention. Until social, political, and economic change provided for a middle class, one of these two extremes — either fancy or plain, either rich or poor — described most historic pieces. Styles of the plainer vernacular or country furniture, though often difficult to identify, persisted much longer than high style goods in fashion-conscious palaces and cities.

Industrialization in the nineteenth century provided a third category of furniture production and consumption. Still made of wood, this machine-made furniture supplied the new middle class with the good, the bad, and the ugly. Emphasis was placed on manufacture rather than on design, because it was acceptable to copy existing styles made available through books and printed drawings. Machinery could and did turn out historic ornament that was arbitrarily applied to equally arbitrary forms. This democratization of design gone amuck inspired reform movements such as the Arts & Crafts. Though intended to elevate popular tastes, reform styles were not for everyone. The market in later nineteenth-century America had broadened to concurrently support endless combinations of historicism as well as so-called "honest" furniture embodying Arts & Crafts ideals; there were also elegantly simple and functional furnishings, including the first built-ins, built by the Shakers throughout the century; and since the mid-1800s, Michael Thonet had produced economical bent wood furniture ranging from the appropriately Victorian to a simplicity that anticipated, as well as influenced, modernism. While the eclectic decades of the late nineteenth century produced some of the most bizarre examples of tongue-in-cheek historicism, they also saw the beginnings of modernism through the eyes of visionary designers such as Charles Rennie Mackintosh and Frank Lloyd Wright (though neither of these architects appeared to value human comfort).

While glimpses of modern style were previewed earlier, Modernism developed in the twentieth century, because style was only part of the story. A zealous attitude toward the use of new machinery and materials was developed at the Bauhaus in Germany and by a new group of professionals in the United States called industrial designers. Popular perceptions of progress, marketing propaganda, and the reality of the Great Depression enabled the new system of mass production to become an alternative to both handicraft and the tiresome generic historic reproductions in the 1920s and 1930s.

The first industrial designers, with backgrounds in art and advertising more often than in engineering, joined industry to offer affordable, alluring, streamlined products to a mass market. Most designers of modern furniture came with architectural training and joined design staffs of companies or worked like the new consultant industrial designers. Techniques for bending plywood splints for the U.S. Navy were the basis for modern furniture designed by Charles and Ray Eames; creative applications for wire accommodated designs by Warren Platner and Harry Bertoia; technologies for molding plastics and fiberglass enabled the success of designs by Eero Saarinen, Eames, and others; Gilbert Rohde and George Nelson's ideas for sectional and modular furniture and the new science of ergonomics were some of the solutions to the problems that faced designers and manufacturers of modern furniture.

Problems of taste were another matter.

As P. T. Barnum reportedly said, "You'll never get rich trying to educate American taste." Modern furniture could not be called popular, in the sense of enjoying wide acceptance. It was appropriate for the times, but that did not prevent the majority from furnishing their homes with mass-produced furniture in historic styles and in no styles. Like buildings without architects, furniture without designers was made by those who tried to copy both past designs and the new modern ones.

The following list of designers and makers includes some of the names of those who have left a legacy of forms, materials, and technologies of circa Fifties furniture and have made them accessible. European names, particularly Scandinavian and Italian, are included, but focus is on the United States. Until this time, the United States had been more of a follower than a leader in the story of Western furniture. The birth of industrial design gave the United States a head start in the arena of mass produced modern furniture. Though clearly influenced by both Bauhaus and Scandinavian Modern designs, the new applications and interpretations have been original. Called "organic design" after the 1940 exhibit by that name at the Museum of Modern Art in New York, its goal was to create a harmonious organization of parts. Without unnecessary ornament, its beauty depended on

exquisitely simple forms that both followed and preceded function. Perhaps for the first time in the history of style, designs intended for both elite and popular audiences and pieces that were neither one-of-a-kind nor crafted by traditional methods could stand on their own.

Many of these classic designs produced by the star companies, Herman Miller and Knoll, have stood on their own in museums and in production lines since their introductions. "If Herman Miller may be thought of as a uniquely American corporation founded by Americans to produce designs by Americans, Knoll Associates was the opposite. That company, founded by Europeans, was to depend heavily, at least at the onset, on foreign designers" (Pulos 83). Having passed the proverbial test of time, these classics have stood on the merits of good design — measured by both aesthetics and function. Many were shown in "Good Design" exhibits held at both the Museum of Modern Art in New York and at the Chicago Merchandise Mart. As George Nelson had already observed in 1949, "There has probably never been a period in the history of furniture when there was so much variety in design, when so many kinds of shapes, materials, and techniques were being explored." Some have been produced continuously, and others have been recently reissued because of growing interest in and appreciation of modernism, especially mid-century design. Ironically, Modern may have become another period style.

Alvar Aalto (1898-1976) Finland

One of the leading Scandinavian modernist architects and town planners, Alvar Aalto became known for the use of laminated bent plywood furniture. He believed that warm wood is preferable to cold metal. He was born in Kuortane, a small town in Finland. After joining the battle for Finnish independence from Russia, he graduated from the Helsinki Institute of Technology in 1921. After serving in the military, he opened his own architectural office in 1923; in 1924 he married architect Aino Marsio, who joined his practice. (She died in 1949, and Aalto married architect Elissa Makiniemi in 1952, and they practiced together for the rest of his life.) Aalto influenced Finnish building practices by helping to form the Finnish Standardization Institute. Impressed by Marcel Breuer, he experimented with tubular metal furniture in the 1920s. Aalto and Finnish designer Otto Korhonen patented a design for plywood, then continued working with formed laminated plywood in designs suited for mass production, including stackable furniture. They eventually improved the process of wood lamination by developing the multi-planar process.

Aalto's participation in the Milan Triennale and the London furniture exhibition in 1933 established his international reputation as a furniture designer. He went on to win numerous international awards, and his work was exhibited alone or with others in museums throughout Europe and the United States. In 1935 he and associates established Artek for the international distribution of his plywood furniture. Among his many furniture designs, the Cantilevered armchair of 1946 and the Fan Leg stool of 1954 are considered modernist classics. Other important designs include the Paimio arm chair of 1931; the Viipuri Collection of 1933 through 1935; the Serving cart in 1936; the bent knee or L-leg; the Y-leg in 1947; and the Fan Leg or X-leg stool in 1954. Furniture was only part of his contribution to modern design, which in addition to architecture, included lighting and glassware. He also taught at MIT from 1940 to 1949. (Cyran "Aalto;" Eidelberg 359; Gandy; Schildt)

Eero Aarnio (b. 1932) Finland

Born in Helsinki, Eero Aarnio was trained at the School of Industrial Arts in Helsinki from 1954 to 1957. In the 1960s he experimented with plastics and opened his own design studio in Helsinki in 1962. His designs were produced in plastic and in steel by the Finnish firm Asko, a major Scandinavian furniture manufacturer. In addition to furniture design, he worked in interior design, industrial design, graphic design, and photography. In 1968 he received the American Industrial Design award for his Pastilli or Gyro chair. Other memorable '60s furniture included the Mushroom chair in 1965, the Bubble chair in 1965, Kantarelli table in 1965, and the Ball or Globe chair in 1966. He then returned to the use of wood and other traditional materials for his later work. (Eidelberg 359; Fiell, *Chairs*; Hiesinger 307-8)

Artek OY Finland

Artek (art + tek for technology) was formed in Helsinki in 1935 by partners Nils-Gustav Hahl and Maire Gullichsen and Alvar and Aino Aalto as the principal share holders. It was intended as a cultural center to promote design through exhibitions and educational programs. Although Artek never became the museum of modern art and design or the publisher of radical art literature that its founders had hoped for, it did become an excellent furniture company with an art gallery. Their major source of income was in the wholesale and retail sales of Aalto's plywood furniture and other interior design products, such as lighting, and they expanded with United States distribution after the war. An American affiliated firm, Artek-Pascoe maintained a shop in New York City to distribute the Aalto designs, but Pascoe eventually dropped the association; Scandinavian Design, also in New York City, became the United States distributor, which I.F.C. later took charge of. By the 1970s, Artek expanded to include numerous international markets. (Eidelberg 161; Schildt 121-28; Stimpson)

Artifort Netherlands

The firm of Artifort in Maastricht, The Netherlands, has been the manufacturer for most of the biomorphic designs by Pierre Paulin, notably the Tongue chair and Ribbon chair, sculptural upholstered forms on foam and metal frames. Artifort also made the Cleopatra sculptural sofa and Chair 506 designed by Geoffrey Harcourt in the 1960s, as well as other seating. (Byars 31)

Artluce Italy

Founded in Milan, Italy, in 1946, Artluce produced modern lamps and lighting. Their flamboyant yet functional light sculptures became a hallmark of Italian design in the 1950s. The first designer was Gino Sarfatti. Other Italian lighting designers associated with the firm include Cini Boeri, Livio Castiglioni, Gianfranco Frattini, King Miranda, and Vittorio Vigano. (Julier 24; Pile 15)

La Ruspa lamp designed by Gae Aulenti, on Alexander Girard table.

Gae Aulenti (b. 1927) Italy

An architect and a professor also known for furniture and other designs, Gae Aulenti studied architecture in Milan, Italy, and graduated in 1954. Her lamp designs include La Ruspa in the 1960s. Important furniture includes Melograno Acerbo, a convertible armchair and sofa for Casa Nova; lounge chair, laminated plywood chairs, and coffee table for Knoll; several tubular steel chairs, sofas, and stools for the companies Zanotta and Poltronova; and aluminum furniture for Zanotta. The same Thonet model that inspired Nelson's Pretzel chair can also be seen in Aulenti's Solus chair in 1967, a plastic-coated tubular steel frame with a round padded seat. In addition to being a furniture designer, Aulenti is an interior designer, industrial designer, a stage designer, and an exhibition designer for Fiat and for Olivetti. She also designed showrooms for Knoll in Boston, New York, and Milan. (Emery 29; Julier 27; Stimpson 137)

Harry Bertoia (1915-1978) Italy; United States

Born in San Lorenzo, Italy, Harry Bertoia came to the United States in 1930 and studied at the Art School of the Society of Arts and Crafts in Detroit (1936-1937). After receiving a scholarship and studying at Cranbrook Academy of Art in 1937, he stayed at Cranbrook to teach metalwork from 1938 to 1943. Due to metal shortages of the war, the metal shop closed, and Bertoia taught graphic art during the years 1942 and 1943. He then moved to California and worked briefly with Charles and Ray Eames designing furniture. In 1943 he married Brigetta Valentiner, daughter of the director of the Detroit Institute of Arts, and in 1946 he became a United States citizen.

Some of Bertoia's most significant contributions to modern design include a line of metal wire furniture for Knoll Associates in the early 1950s. His Diamond chair and Bird chair based on wire grids were introduced in 1952; he then stayed with Knoll as a consultant. In 1954 Bertoia won a Gold Medal from the Architectural League of New York for a steel screen combined with other metals for Manufacturers Hanover Trust Co. Other awards include a Gold Medal in 1973 from the American Institute of Architects, and the Academy Institute Award in 1975 from the American Academy of Letters. (Detroit 268; Eidelberg 363; Larrabee)

Marcel Breuer (1902-1981) Hungary; United States

Marcel Breuer is best known for the introduction of tubular steel furniture for interiors, notably the Bauhaus-designed Wassily chair of 1925, which has been reintroduced by Knoll.

United States Patent Office drawing of "Diamond" chair designed by Harry Bertoia for Knoll, filed July 23, 1952.

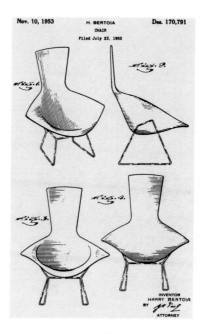

United States Patent Office drawing of "Bird" chair designed by Harry Bertoia for Knoll, filed July 23, 1952.

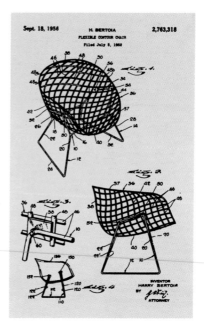

United States Patent Office drawing of flexible contour chair designed by Harry Bertoia for Knoll, filed July 5, 1952.

His cantilevered Cesca chair of 1928, which combines steel, wood, and cane, has become one of the most influential twentieth-century chair designs and is still being produced by Thonet. Other designs include the Aluminum chair in 1933 and Isokon lounge chair in 1935. Though not generally well known for his Fifties designs, Breuer's early classic chair designs have enjoyed continuous popularity in both residential and public interiors, adding to the significance of his contribution to modern design.

Born in Pécs, Hungary, Breuer studied at the Vienna Academy of Fine Art and at the Weimar Bauhaus from 1920 to 1924, where he became a master of the furniture workshop. After the Bauhaus moved to Dessau in 1925, he remained for two more years. He opened his own architectural office in Berlin (1928-1931) and then in London from 1935 to 1937. At the invitation of Walter Gropius in 1937, Breuer emigrated to the United States and became an associate professor at the School of Design at Harvard University from 1937 to 1946. Also during those years he had an architectural practice with Gropius in Cambridge, Massachusetts (1937-1941). In 1946 he headed his own firm of Marcel Breuer & Associates in New York City and retired in 1976. (Gandy; Wilk)

Lightolier table lamp with porcelain base designed by Georges Briard and made by Hyalyn. *Photo courtesy Georges Briard.*

Georges Briard (b. 1917) Russia; United States

Born in the Russian Ukraine, Jascha Brojdo moved to Poland at the age of four and came to the United States in the late 1930s. After earning a degree from the University of Chicago and Art Institute of Chicago joint program, he served in United States Army Intelligence. After his Army discharge, he hand decorated metal trays. Since commercial art was not necessarily part of Brojdo's artistic goals, he suggested to his employer, Max Wille, that he use a designer pseudonym, hence the name Georges Briard. Their company would be called Georges Briard Designs/M. Wille Inc.

Briard decided to use 22-karat gold to decorate bent flat glass. The Bent Glass Co. already made this for ceiling light fixtures, and they formed what would become the very successful Glass Guild in Jamaica, New York to manufacture and market the new product. Collaboration with many other companies included Woodland in Glen Falls, New York, which made high quality wood products. In the early 1960s, Hyalyn Porcelain in Hickory, North Carolina had Briard design modern shapes for a line of bisque items with lavish gold decorations that epitomized Briard's style; he called the series "Midas." Hyalyn also used Briard's raised gold motifs on porcelain lamp bases produced for Lightolier of Secaucus, New Jersey.

After a decade of near magical success, by the mid-1960s Georges Briard Designs discontinued many of their popular lines. These were replaced by melamine dinnerware, ice buckets and other barware, and fine china dinnerware in the 1970s and 1980s. The company closed in 1989. (Piña)

Cassina Italy

One of the first Italian furniture companies to produce modern designs for an international market, Cassina was founded in 1927 by Cesare Cassina and his brother Umberto in Meda, a suburb of Milan, Italy. Before 1940 they

catered to popular tastes, but after the war they produced new designs by Italian modernists Franco Albini and Mario Bellini. During the years 1947-1952 a huge order from the Italian Navy required new production facilities. That, plus the guaranteed revenues from the order enabled Cassina to develop their new modern design philosophy. In addition to Bellini, other important designers in the 1950s included Carlo De Carli, Gianfranco Frattini, Vico Magistretti, Ico Parisi, Nino Zancada, and Gio Ponti. Significant designs include Ponti's Distex chair in 1953 and Superleggera chair (engineered by Fausto Redaelli) from 1952 on. In addition to Bellini and Magistretti, Tobia and Afra Scarpa designed in the 1960s; Gaetano Pesce worked in the 1970s. The company also reintroduced Frank Lloyd Wright's Robie chairs, Allen table, Midway chair, and Barrel chair as well as early classics by Mackintosh, Rietveld, and the Le Corbusier/Jeanneret/Perriand 1920s designs of Grand Confort chairs and sofa from 1965 on. (Julier 47; Santini; Sparke *Italian*)

Robin Day (b. 1915) England

A furniture and industrial designer, Robin Day, along with Clive Latimer, won first prize for Low-Cost Furniture Design in the 1948 competition by the Museum of Modern Art in New York. Their prize-winning tapered wooden and tubular metal storage units led to Day's collaboration with Hille, one of Britain's leading contract furniture manufacturers, in 1949. Day designed primarily for molded plastic, plywood, and upholstered metal frames. He is known for the 1963 Poly or Polyprop stacking chair, a single piece polypropylene shell, available in a variety of colors, on a tubular steel frame. Day also designed aircraft interiors, carpets, and exhibitions. (Dormer 82; Fiell, *Chairs*; Pile 62)

Donald Deskey (1894-1989) United States
Though known for his dazzling Art Deco designs and participation in the early stages of American modernism, his career included mid-century designs as well. Donald Deskey was one of the first to integrate modern art into advertising design and manufactured products and was also one of the first to introduce tubular steel furniture in the United States. Originally from Minnesota, he studied at Mark Hopkins Institute (California School of Fine Arts), the University of California at Berkeley, and in Paris. After serving in the military, he moved to New York City in 1921 to work in advertising, but since his work was considered too modern, he opened his own agency. After traveling to Paris twice and seeing the 1925 Decorative Arts Exhibition, he worked in the Art Moderne style for stage sets, furniture, and screens. Deskey

was a founding member and exhibiter of the American Designers' Gallery in 1928 and 1929, and the American Union of Decorative Artists and Craftsmen in 1930 and 1931. Best known for the interior of Radio City Music Hall, he also developed a striated fir plywood called Weldtex, did the first modern interior for an American ocean liner, the S. S. Argenta, and designed items such as pianos, billiard tables, clocks, office equipment, silverware, oil burners, radios, glassware, and slot machines, as well as package designs for Procter & Gamble. His 1950 design for the Crest toothpaste package is still in use. (Hiesinger 325; Pile 65; Pulos)

Henry Dreyfuss (1904-1972) United States
Along with other pioneer modernists, Henry Dreyfuss contributed to mid-century design as well. He was born in New York, and without formal design training became one of the first major industrial designers. After working for Norman Bel Geddes in the 1920s and designing sets, costumes, and lighting for the Strand Theater in New York, he opened his own design office in 1929. One of his earliest and longest lasting clients was Bell Telephone Laboratories. He was a consultant designer for A T & T from 1930, John Deere & Co. (1937), Hyster (1951), Poleroid (1961), and American Airlines (1963). Dreyfuss collaborated on the model city

at the 1939 New York World's Fair; he redesigned the cars of the New York Railroad's Mercury in 1936, the 20th Century Limited in 1938, and airplane interiors for American Airlines, Lockheed, and Pan Am. He was interested in human values, pioneered the field of ergonomics, and wrote books including *Designing for People* in 1955 and *Measure of Man* in 1959. (Eidelberg 370; Julier 73; Pulos)

Dunbar Furniture Corp. United States

In 1919 Riney Dunbar's Buggy Works in Linn Grove, Illinois, began furniture manufacture under the name Dunbar Furniture Inc. in Berne, Indiana. A new plant was added in 1920 and a showroom in 1927. The versatile and prolific designer Edward J. Wormley began as design director in 1931. In the late 1930s Dunbar produced two distinctly different lines of furniture — traditional and modern (Swedish). Wormley was responsible for an average of 100 designs each year, and many of his early pieces remained in production for decades. One of his most important projects for the company was his 150-piece Janus Collection with an Arts & Crafts influence, in 1957. Wormley remained with the company until 1968. Dunbar also produced chairs and sofas by Michael Graves recalling the streamlined style of the 1930s, and in the 1980s produced the Keps Bay sofa for John Saladino. (Eidelberg 371; Stimpson 186)

Charles Ormand Eames (1907-1978) United States

Born in St. Louis, Missouri, Charles Eames studied architecture at Washington University in St. Louis from 1925 through 1928. After marrying Catherine Dewey Woermann, he traveled in Europe in 1929. He was a partner in the architectural firm Gray and Eames (later with Pauly) in St. Louis from 1930 through 1933, and lived in Mexico in 1934. Then from 1934 to 1938 he was a partner in the firm Eames and Walsh. After studying at the Cranbrook Academy of Art on scholarship (1938-1939), Eames taught at Cranbrook from 1939 to 1941, while also working for Eliel and Eero Saarinen.

In 1941 Eames divorced Catherine to marry Ray Kaiser. The couple moved to Los Angeles and developed new techniques for molding plywood. The new husband and wife partnership would be the source of significant modern design under the name the Offices of Charles and Ray Eames. He was awarded the Kaufmann International Design Award in 1961, an American Institute of Architects Award in 1977, and the Queen's Gold Medal for Architecture in London, posthumously in 1979. (Detroit; Neuhart)

Composite photo of experimental chair designs by Charles and Ray Eames. *Photo ©1993 Sotheby's, Inc., courtesy Sotheby's New York.*

Charles and Ray Eames (Offices of) United States

After architect Charles Ormand Eames married artist Ray Kaiser, they formed a design partnership that became an important source of modern design from 1941 to 1978. Some of their work includes: 1941-1942 developed plywood splints for the United States Navy, formed the Plyformed Wood Co. which later became the Molded Plywood Division of Evans Products; 1945 experimented with plywood chairs, children's furniture, and tables; 1946 Eames plywood furniture exhibit in New York brought Evans Products into the furniture business, and Herman Miller was granted exclusive marketing and distribution rights for Eames plywood furniture; Eames was a major source of Herman Miller furniture designs such as the 1946 LCM dining chair, DCW molded plywood chair, and the plywood Folding Screen; 1950 Storage units; 1950-1953 DAR Shell chairs; 1951-1953 Wire mesh chairs, DKR Shell chair, and wire sofa; 1953 Hang-It-All; 1954 Compact sofa and Stadium seating; 1955 Stacking chair; 1956 Lounge chair and ottoman; 1958 Aluminum Group furniture; 1960 Time-Life chair and stool; 1961 La Fonda chair and Contract storage; 1962 Tandem Sling seating; 1963 Tandem Shell seating; 1964 3473 Sofa; 1964-1965 Segmented base tables; 1968 Chaise; 1969 Soft Pad group; 1970 Drafting chair; 1971 Two-piece Plastic chair and the Loose Cushion Armchair. They also designed The Toy in 1951, House of Cards 1952, and Giant House of Cards 1953; they designed the IBM Corp. Pavilion at the 1964 New York World's Fair, Herman Miller showrooms, other exhibits, graphics, houses, they did photography, and made many films from 1946 to 1978. (Kirkham; Neuhart)

Ray Kaiser Eames (1912-1938) United States

Ray Kaiser was born in Sacramento, California. She attended the May Friend Bennett School in Millbrook, New Jersey, from 1931 through 1933, then at the Art Students League in New York before studying painting at the Hans Hoffman School from 1933 through 1939. She attended Cranbrook Academy of Art from 1940 to 1941 and then married Charles Eames. Although some work, such as designs for covers of *Art & Architecture* magazine in the early 1940s, was individual, most of her work was in partnership with her husband in the Offices of Charles and Ray Eames from 1941 to 1978. After Charles died in 1978, she continued their work in what is considered to be one of the greatest husband and wife design collaborations of the century. (Kirkham; Neuhart)

Eames molded plywood furniture for Herman Miller, 1946. *Photo Charles Eames, courtesy Herman Miller.*

Bird's-eye view of other Eames molded furniture, a version of the photo used in a 1948 Herman Miller advertisement. *Photo Charles Eames, courtesy Herman Miller.*

Evans Products Co., Molded Plywood Division United States

In 1941 Charles and Ray Eames and three colleagues established the Plyformed Wood Co. in West Los Angeles. After getting the United States Navy contract for plywood splints, the company moved to nearby Venice, California. In 1943 Edward Evans, head of Evans Products Co. in Detroit bought the rights to produce and distribute the Plyformed Wood splints, and the company was renamed Molded Plywood Division, a subsidiary of Evans Products.

When the Eameses began to make chairs and other furniture out of plywood, Herman Miller gained exclusive rights to distribute the products in 1946. The next year, the Venice plant closed and moved to Grand Haven, Michigan. Herman Miller purchased the Molded Plywood Division and made the Eames lines under its name. (Eidelberg 387-8; Neuhart 33; Pulos 79)

Paul Frankl (1887-1958) Austria; United States

Paul Frankl was trained in architecture in Berlin, Vienna, Paris, and Munich. He came to the United States in 1914 and worked as a decorator and a furniture designer. Frankl became known for his designs of rectilinear stepped Skyscraper furniture in New York in the 1920s and other Art Deco and modernist work, and in 1930 he published the book *Form and Re-Form*.

After the war he relocated to California and practiced interior design using a simple geometric style called California Modern. His biomorphic coffee table for Johnson Furniture is atypical of Frankl's better known angular style. (Hiesinger 330; Pile 86)

Frank O. Gehry (b. 1930) Canada

Born Frank Goldberg in Toronto, Frank Gehry studied architecture at the University of Southern California in Los Angeles from 1949 through 1951 and 1954 and then at Harvard Graduate School of Design from 1956 through 1957. He worked for Victor Gruen Associates in Los Angeles and for André Remondet in Paris before establishing his own architectural office in Los Angeles in 1962. One of his many architectural commissions was the Vitra Design Museum, Weil am Rhein, Germany. His designs are considered to be eccentric, and along with similar architecture of the 1970s, has been given names such as "ad hoc" or "punk" design. His Easy Edges epoxy-laminated cardboard chairs of 1971, originally produced by the Swiss firm Cheru Enterprises, are considered to exemplify "ad hoc" design and brought him international recognition. Gehry later designed a series of bentwood furniture for Knoll (1989-1991). He is a Fellow of the American Institute of Architects and won the Pritzker Architecture Prize in 1989. (Byars 210; Pile 93-4; Stimpson 157)

Alexander Girard fabrics with Herman Miller furniture. *Photo courtesy Herman Miller.*

Alexander Girard (1907-1993) United States

Born in New York, Alexander Girard was trained in architecture in London, Florence, Rome, and New York. He opened his own design office in New York in 1932 and then in Detroit in 1937, where he practiced architecture and interior design. Commissions included design of automobile interiors for Ford Motor Co. and interiors and radio cabinet designs for Detrola Corp. In 1938 he designed his own home in Grosse Pointe, Michigan, and filled it with folk art from around the world, the inspiration for all of his future designs. In 1949 Girard organized "An Exhibition for Modern Living" for the Detroit Institute of Arts. He joined Herman Miller in 1950 and became the first director of design for the new textile division and director of upholstery in 1952, and he developed new weaves, prints, and color lines. He also designed the Herman Miller Showroom in San Francisco in 1959 and collaborated with Eames on a line of furniture for the New York restaurant La Fonda del Sol. Girard developed a corporate identity program for Braniff International in 1964 using differently colored aircraft. (Abercrombie 103; Julier 92; Pile 99)

Fritz Hansen Furniture Denmark

Fritz Hansen was a cabinetmaker who started a business in Denmark in 1872 special-

Chair designed by Alexander Girard. *Photo courtesy Treadway Gallery.*

izing in wood turning. The company of Fritz Hansen became interested in bentwood furniture and hired architects in the 1930s to design it, and in 1932 began a relationship with Arne Jacobsen. Fritz Hansen produced his designs, such as the plywood and chromed stacking chair beginning in 1951, the Ant chair, a simple dining chair of pressed wood and fiberglass in 1952, molded plywood chair from 1955 on, the Swan upholstered armchair from 1957 on, and the Egg chair and ottoman, also beginning in 1957. The company also produced the work of many other modern designers such as Kaare Klint's Church chair in 1936 and Hans Wegner's Peacock chair in 1947. (Dormer 127; Sparke *Furniture* 62)

Geoffrey Harcourt (b. 1935) England

Geoffrey Harcourt studied at High Wycombe and at the Royal College of Art. He spent a year in the United States and then joined the Artifort Design Group. His comfortable 1960s designs include Chair 506 fully upholstered tilted chair on a pedestal, and the Cleopatra sofa, a sculptural form of upholstered molded foam. (Stimpson 147)

Irving Harper (b. 1916) United States

Irving Harper studied at Brooklyn College, Pratt Institute, and Cooper Union Architectural School, graduating in 1938. He worked for the industrial design offices of both Gilbert Rohde and Raymond Lowey before joining George Nelson Associates. Harper is credited with the designs of the famous Ball Clock of 1948 produced by the Howard Miller Clock Co., many of the eighty pieces in Nelson's first Herman Miller Collection in 1946, the upholstered seating system in 1950, the Marshmallow Sofa in 1956, and other designs produced by Herman Miller. In 1963 he joined Philip George in the firm Harper and George and designed graphics and interiors for Braniff Airlines and Pennsylvania Central Railroad. Harper is still an independent designer. (Abercrombie; Pile 114)

Eames folding screen on display at Herman Miller Pavilion furniture showroom, Grandville, Michigan.

Herman Miller United States

The Star Furniture Co. was founded in Zeeland, Michigan, in 1905 by Herman Miller and others to produce high quality furniture, especially bedroom suites, in historic revival styles. Dirk Jan De Pree began as a clerk in 1909 and became president of the company by 1919, when it was renamed the Michigan Star Furniture Co. DePree and his father-in-law, Herman Miller purchased 51% of the stock in 1923 and renamed the company Herman Miller Furniture Co. In 1969 it became Herman Miller, Inc.

Until 1930 the company produced only wood traditional furniture. With the shrinking market of the Depression, they hired Gilbert Rohde and reluctantly took a chance with modern design. Rohde helped turn the company in a totally new direction, and in 1933 its modern furniture debut was held at the Century of Progress exposition in Chicago. A showroom in the Chicago Merchandise Mart opened in 1939, and another opened in New York in 1941. Herman Miller entered the office furniture market in 1942 with its modular Executive Office Group (EOG) system designed by Rohde. When Rohde died in 1944 his replacement for mod-

Herman Miller furniture grouping of Surfboard table, Aluminum Group chairs, and marble-top table, all designed by Charles and Ray Eames. *Photo Marvin Rand, courtesy Herman Miller.*

Chair display at Herman Miller Pavilion furniture showroom. *Photo courtesy Herman Miller.*

ern design was architect George Nelson, who was hired in 1946 and carried on with the EOG concept. In addition to Nelson's enormous personal contribution over the next four decades, he helped to bring in other designers. Isamu Noguchi is known for his Biomorphic coffee table of 1947; Charles and Ray Eames popularized many designs for molded plywood and plastics; Alexander Girard designed textiles. Another important name is Robert Probst, head of Herman Miller Research division, formed in 1960, and inventor of the Action Office. Designs for Action Office I (1964-1970) and Action Office II (1968-1976) were by the George Nelson office. Other furniture designers included Poul Kjaerholm, Fritz Haller, and Verner Panton. Although original mid-century classics and those reissued as part of the "herman miller for the home" collection have been used in residences, the focus of Herman Miller has been and is today on modern office environments. Belief in the importance of good design, honest products, and respect for individuals and the environment have been driving forces. As Hugh De Pree said, "Herman Miller has always operated with the designer as the creative force. Perhaps the most important consequence of that force has been the design of Herman Miller itself" (Caplan 119). (Caplan, Herman Miller Archives)

herman miller for the home Platform bench, originally called a Slat bench until 1961, designed by George Nelson. *Photo Phil Schaafsma, courtesy Herman Miller.*

Heywood-Wakefield grouping with chests and round
cocktail table. *Courtesy Studio Moderne.*

Heywood-Wakefield United States

In 1826 five Heywood brothers began to make chairs in a barn in Gardner, Massachusetts, and in 1835 formed B. F. Heywood & Co. The name changed to Heywood & Wood in 1844, Heywood Chair Manufacturing Co. in 1851, and Heywood Brothers & Co. in 1861. By 1896 they had three factories and eight warehouses and the product included reed and rattan furniture, wooden school desks, and train seating.

When the Lloyd Manufacturing Co., producer of tubular metal items and woven baby carriages, was acquired in 1921, they became reincorporated as Heywood-Wakefield Co. Gilbert Rohde, who brought modern design to Herman Miller in 1930, also worked to develop a modern line at Heywood-Wakefield in the early 1930s, followed by Russel Wright for a brief time. By 1935 the first Streamlined Modern design was introduced by Heywood-Wakefield, and modern designers Leo Jiranek and Count Alexis de Sakhnoffsky designed for them. By 1940 the modern light furniture with rounded corners, smooth edges, and pieces bent from solid wood was the fastest selling modern furniture in America. But in the 1950s financial problems mounted, and by the 1960s their Modern lines were phased out. In 1979 production stopped in all but two plants, and in 1987 the company filed for bankruptcy. Their thirty years of modern wood furniture production have left many classics of mid-century design, some of which are being reissued today by the reopened Heywood-Wakefield Company. (Rouland)

Wolfgang Hoffmann (1900-1969) Austria; United States

Wolfgang Hoffmann was the son of Viennese architect and Wiener Werkstätte leader Josef Hoffmann (1870-1956). He was born in Vienna, where he studied architecture at the School of Arts and Crafts. In 1925, he and his wife, designer Pola Hoffmann, moved to the United States and worked briefly for Joseph Urban and for Elly Jacques Kahn. Hoffmann is known for his tubular steel chairs made by Howell Company in Geneva, Illinois in the 1930s. He moved to Illinois in 1933 to design exclusively for Howell. From 1933 to 1942 his S-chairs used for dinette sets in small kitchens or in combination living/dining rooms were very successful. He patented several tubular metal chair designs and numerous smoking stands. Much of the popular mass produced tubular steel furniture seen today was designed by Hoffman and made by Howell. (Byars 261-2; Sparke *Furniture* 41)

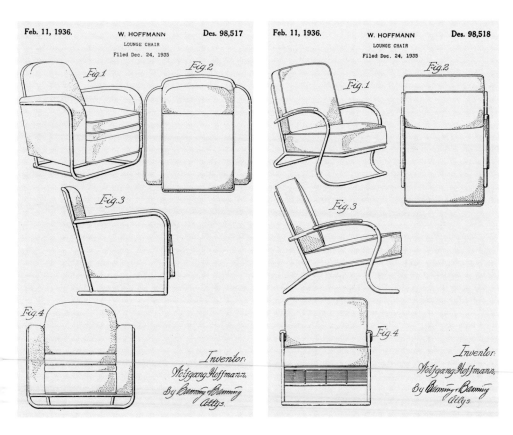

Feb. 11, 1936.   W. HOFFMANN   Des. 98,517
LOUNGE CHAIR
Filed Dec. 24, 1935

Fig.1   Fig.2
Fig.3
Fig.4

Inventor.
Wolfgang Hoffmann.
By Banning & Banning
Attys.

Feb. 11, 1936.   W. HOFFMANN   Des. 98,518
LOUNGE CHAIR
Filed Dec. 24, 1935

Fig.1   Fig.2
Fig.3
Fig.4

Inventor.
Wolfgang Hoffmann.
By Banning & Banning
Attys.

United States Patent Office drawings
of chairs designed by Wolfgang
Hoffmann, filed December 24, 1935.

Howard Miller Clock Co.   United States

The Herman Miller Clock Co. was founded in Zeeland, Michigan, in 1926 by Herman Miller's son Howard, who was then general manager of Colonial Manufacturing, and maker of grandfather clocks. The company reorganized and changed its name to the Howard Miller Clock Co. in the 1930s, and in 1939 they introduced the first modern lines at the New York World's Fair. After the war George Nelson Associates designed a series of modern clocks without numbers that have become symbols of mid-century design, notably the Ball clock of 1948. Nelson also designed the famous Bubble lamps made of plastic sprayed onto a wire frame, which was also produced by Howard Miller from 1952. After these modern designs of the 1950s and 1960s, the company returned to its focus on traditional items such as grandfather clocks and alarm clocks. In 1983 they purchased the Hekman Furniture Co. in Grand Rapids; in 1989, under the direction of Howard Miller's son Philip, they introduced a line of wooden curio cabinets resembling clock cases without clocks. The manufacturing facility in Zeeland, which opened in 1966, is considered one of the most efficient production plants in the industry. (Eidelberg 376; Kaskovich; Miller)

Ball clock, model #4755 designed by George Nelson Associates for Howard Miller, birch "atom" balls on brass spokes, brass central disc, black hands.

Arne Jacobsen (1902-1971) Denmark

Arne Jacobsen was born in Copenhagen, was trained as a mason at the School of Applied Arts in Copenhagen from 1917 to 1924 and then studied architecture at the Royal Danish Academy of Arts in Copenhagen, graduating in 1927. After working in the architectural office of Paul Holsoe from 1927 to 1930 he established his own office, which he headed until he died in 1971. In addition to working independently as an architect and a designer of furniture, he designed textiles, carpets, stainless steel flatware, glassware, ceramics, lighting fixtures, bathroom fixtures, and interiors. From 1956 on, he was professor of architecture at the Royal Academy of Art in Copenhagen. In addition to architectural work, such as St. Catherine College at Oxford, Rødovre Town Hall, Royal Hotel Copenhagen, the SAS Hotel in Copenhagen, houses, schools, and factories, he is known for his furniture design for Fritz Hansen of Allerød, Denmark. His three-legged molded plywood chair in 1952 is considered to have been a turning point in Danish Modern furniture design. Other important Fifties designs include elegantly simple pressure-molded beech plywood chairs, such as the Ant chair in 1955. The classic Swan chair and settee and the Egg chair designed in 1957 have been produced continuously since their introduction. Among his awards is a silver medal at the 1957 Milan Triennale. (Eidelberg 377; Fehrman 52-6; Zahle)

Egg chair designed by Arne Jacobsen and made by Fritz Hansen, c. 1957, blue cloth upholstery. *Photo courtesy Skinner, Inc.*

Pierre Jeanneret (1896-1967) Switzerland

Born in Geneva, Pierre Jeanneret studied architecture at L'Ecole des Beaux-Arts from 1913 to 1915 and again from 1918 to 1921. He worked with the Perret brothers until 1923 and then collaborated with his cousin Charles Edouard Jeanneret (Le Corbusier) from 1923 to 1940 as a quiet partner playing a significant behind-the-scenes role in Le Corbusier's architecture. Furniture designs include the Grand Confort chairs and sofa in International Style, originally made by Gebrüder Thonet and reissued by Cassina in Italy from 1965. Jeanneret also worked with Jean Prouvé, Charlotte Perriand, Georges Blanchon, and A. Masson. From 1951 through 1965 he was involved in architecture and directed the School of Architecture at Chandigarh, India. While in India, he experimented with low-cost furniture made of native materials such as cord and bamboo. (Fiell, *Chairs*; Hiesinger 345)

Leo Jiranek United States

Leo Jiranek studied engineering at Princeton and graduated in 1922. In 1934 he and Donald Deskey formed a short-lived company called Amodec Inc. to manufacture modern furniture designs. He worked for Heywood-Wakefield as a design consultant from 1935 into the 1950s designing their Modern line, rattan

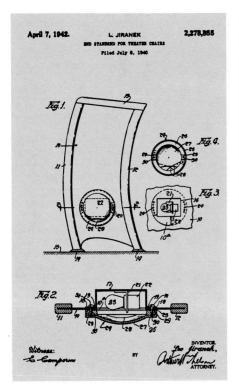

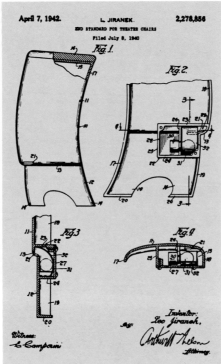

United States Patent Office drawings of end standard for theater chairs designed by Leo Jiranek for Heywood-Wakefield, filed July 8, 1940.

summer furniture, theater seating, and baby carriages for their Lloyd Division. As a leading furniture designer, he was one of the organizers of the American Furniture Mart Designers Institute in 1936, which changed to American Designers Institute (ADI) in 1939. In 1941 Jiranek chaired the National Emergency Committee of the ADI to help the United States with the war effort in the area of manufacturing and materials shortages. (Pulos 196-7; Rouland 27)

Finn Juhl (1912-1989) Denmark

Finn Juhl studied at the Royal Danish Academy of Fine Arts from 1930 through 1934 and architecture at the Copenhagen Academy of Art. From 1934 to 1945 he practiced architecture, and in 1937 started a collaboration with cabinetmaker Niels Vodder. In 1945 Juhl opened his own office in Copenhagen and began a teaching career, heading the school of House Furnishings (Interior Design) at Frederiksberg (1945-1955).

The 1940s and 1950s were significant for furniture design, and Juhl won 36 prizes in competitions in Copenhagen, plus five gold medals at Milan Triennales in 1954 and 1957. Believing in a strong connection between fine and applied arts, he preferred freeform sculpture, primitive art, and organic architecture and design. His seating designs, crafted by Niels Vodder, represented the organic look in Scandivanian design, exemplified by the Chieftain armchair of 1949. He also designed a series for Baker Furniture in Grand Rapids, Michigan (1949-1951); sofas, chairs, and tables with metal frames for Bovirke in Denmark in 1953; wooden pieces to be mass produced by France & Son in Denmark in the late 1950s; and other items such as glassware. (Eidelberg 378; Julier 109; Zahle 278)

Vladimir Kagan (b. 1927) Germany; United States

States

Vladimir Kagan was born in Worms am Rhein, Germany, and moved to the United States in 1938. He studied architecture at Columbia University in New York City. In 1947 he worked in his father's woodworking shop and soon began to design furniture. When Kagan opened a New York showroom in 1950, he attracted corporate clients including General Motors, Monsanto, Warner Communications, American Express, and Walt Disney; his individual clients included Marilyn Monroe, Xavier Cougat, and Lily Pons. He later established Vladimir Kagan Design Group and became a design consultant to the home furnishings and contract furniture industries, and also designed furniture that was manufactured by several companies. Kagan served as president of the New York chapter of the American Society of Interior Designers, taught at Parsons School of Design, and displayed his work in the 1958 Good Design exhibition at the Museum of Modern Art. Some of his most successful mid-century seating designs have sculpted wood frames and nubby natural colored upholstery. (Byars 288)

Knoll United States

In 1938 Hans Knoll formed the Hans G. Knoll Furniture Co. in New York City. His first modern furniture was a chair designed by Jens

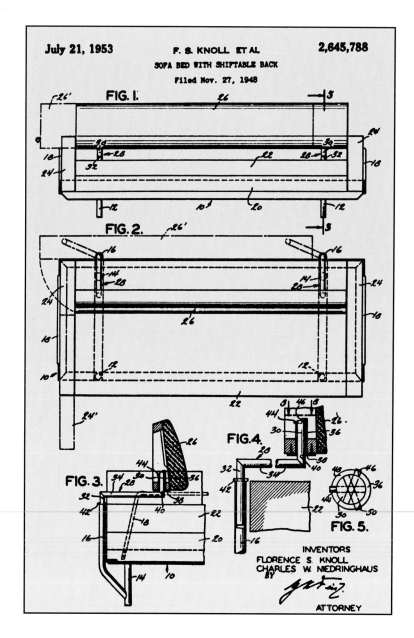

United States Patent Office drawing of sofa bed with shiftable back designed by Florence S. Knoll, filed Nov. 27, 1948.

KnollStudio The Brno Chair

The Brno Chair, Knoll Studio.
Photo courtesy Knoll.

Knoll Studio Saarinen Pedestal Collection.
Photo courtesy Knoll.

Risom in 1941, followed by a line of about fifteen items. In 1943 Florence Schust joined the company. An important early commission was the office of Nelson Rockefeller at Rockefeller Plaza in 1945; in the same year Florence started the Knoll Planning Unit. In 1946 Hans and Florence were married and started Knoll Associates (name used until 1959), and in 1947 the Knoll textile division was formed. The associates were internationally known designers and artists who worked on a royalty basis, and the style tended more toward the Bauhaus than Scandinavia. In 1948 Mies van der Rohe gave Knoll the right to reproduce his Barcelona chair and then Brno and other classics. Other early Knoll designers included Franco Albini, Hans Bellmann, Pierre Jeanneret, Isamu Noguchi, and Eero Saarinen, known best for his Womb chair of 1948 and then Pedestal chairs and tables in 1956. In the early 1950s Harry Bertoia introduced his wire seating.

In 1955 Han Knoll was killed in an automobile accident, and Florence Knoll took over the company, which she sold to Art Metal Inc., an office furniture manufacturer, in 1959. Knoll then became a subsidiary of Walter E. Heller International in 1965. In 1967 they hired Massimo Vignelli to design graphics, and in 1968 Knoll acquired the company Gavina, along with designs by Marcel Breuer, Cini Boeri, Roberto Sebastian Matta, and others. The company name was changed to Knoll International in 1969, although that name had been used in Europe since 1951. Then in 1977 Knoll was acquired by General Felt Industries; from 1990 through 1995 the company went by the name The Knoll Group. Today, Knoll emphasizes office furnishings in the United States, and both office and residential in Europe. (Larrabee)

Florence Schust Knoll (Bassett) (b. 1917)
United States

Born in Saginaw, Michigan, Florence Schust studied at the Cranbrook Academy of Art from 1934 through 1937, with one semester at the Columbia University School of Architecture. She also studied architecture in London from 1938 through 1939 and then worked in the office of Walter Gropius in Cambridge and Marcel Breuer in New York City in 1940. She studied architecture at the Illinois Institute of Technology under Mies van der Rohe from 1940 through 1941.

Schust joined Knoll in 1943 and married Hans Knoll in 1946, and she was considered an arbiter of taste for the company, designing showrooms and controlling overall design from graphics to display. She didn't consider herself a furniture designer, but rather the one to create what she called the "fill-in" pieces that needed to be done but that no one else was designing. She was responsible for "meat and potatoes" case goods and office furniture in the 1950s. When Hans died in 1955, Florence took over the company; when she married Harry Hood Bassett in 1958, she resigned as president and remained as a consultant. Once the heart of Knoll design, Florence Bassett ended the relationship with the company in 1965 and went into private design practice. She was awarded a gold medal from the American Institute of Architects for her role in the service of contemporary architecture in the United States and abroad. (Detroit; Larrabee)

Hans Knoll (1914-1955) Germany; United States

Hans Knoll was born in Stuttgart; his father was a pioneer manufacturer of modern furniture in Weimar and made early Bauhaus furniture for Gropius, Breuer, and Mies. Educated in Switzerland and England, Hans Knoll started Plan Ltd., an interior design firm, in England. In 1937 he went to New York, and in the following year opened his one-room furniture company, Hans G. Knoll Furniture Co. He had two children with his first wife, and then married Florence Schust in 1946. The couple organized Knoll Associates, with Hans as president and Florence as vice-president and direc-

tor of planning. Their company was one of the pioneers of modern furniture in the United States. When Hans was killed in an automobile accident in Havana, Cuba, in 1955, his widow took over as president and owner of Knoll Associates. (Larrabee)

Paul László (1900-1993) Hungary

Born in Budapest, Hungary, Paul László studied architecture in Vienna, Paris, and Berlin. He opened a decorating firm in Vienna in 1923, then in 1927 moved to Stuttgart and established a reputation. In 1936 he moved to Beverly Hills, California, and specialized in modern houses and interiors. Clients included Cary Grant, Barbara Hutton, Barbara Stanwyck, Elizabeth Taylor, and Robert Taylor. He designed stores as well as casinos and showrooms in Howard Hughes' Las Vegas hotels. László designed upholstered pieces and table groups for Herman Miller in the late 1940s, and his chair with matching sofa and circular coffee table were shown in the 1948 Herman Miller catalog. In addition to his architectural and interior design commissions, other designs included custom furniture, textiles, and lamps. (Abercrombie 107; Byars 318; Pile 147)

Laverne Originals United States

Erwine Laverne (b. 1909 New York) and

Estelle Lester Laverne (b. 1915 New York) both studied painting with Hans Hofmann and Kuniyoshi at the Art Students League in New York. They met in 1934, married, and founded a manufacturing and retail wallpaper company called Laverne Originals in 1938, with design studios at the L. C. Tiffany estate in Oyster Bay, New York. They changed the name to Laverne International in 1948, the same year they won the American Fabrics Award at the Metropolitan Museum of Art. Other awards included the Good Design awards from the Museum of Modern Art in 1949 for textiles, 1952 for wall coverings, and 1953 for furniture; and awards by the American Institute of Decorators in 1947, 1949, 1951, 1952, and 1957.

Many artists and designers worked for Laverne Originals, such as Alexander Calder, whose Constellation design for textiles and wall covering resembled George Nelson's famous Ball Clock, William Katavolos, Douglas Kelly, Gyorgy Kepes, Ray Komai, Ross Littell, Alvin Lustig, and Oscar Niemeyer. Their molded furniture was popular with interior designers in the late 1950s, and a series of lucite chair designs in their Invisible Group were produced from 1957 to 1972. (Byars 320; Eidelberg 381-2; Pile 148)

Lightolier United States

The New York Gas Appliance Co. was founded in 1904 by Bernhard Blitzer in New York City. Originally dealing in gas lighting fittings, by 1909 they had moved to electric lighting fixtures. The name was changed to Lightolier in 1918. The building boom of the 1920s enabled Lightolier, under the direction of Bernhard's son Moses D. Blitzer, to expand into the design and manufacture of its products. During the Depression, emphasis was placed on portable lamps, and by the late 1930s Streamlined and other modern styles were introduced by designers Carl Moser and Kurt Versen.

After producing for the U. S. Navy during World War II, the company turned increasingly toward modern design and added designers Gerald Thurston and consultant Edward Wormley. In 1949 William Blitzer (grandson of Bernhard) joined the firm in product development and emphasized modern functional lighting, which soon positioned Lightolier as a leader in the field. Noel Florence, Anthony Donato, and Kingsly Chan joined the design staff for florescent, track, and recessed downlighting; Henry Muller took over much of the decorative design as Moser retired. Although viewing it as a minor segment of the business, Lightolier also continued table lamp production, including (briefly) Georges Briard's Hyalyn designs, until the early 1970s.

Lightolier was owned by the Blitzer family and employees until going public in 1968. It was acquired by Bairnco in 1981, and in 1984, when all of Bairnco's lighting companies spun off into The Genlyte Group, Inc., Lightolier became the major asset of Genlyte. Specializing in interior residential and contract lighting, Lightolier produces modern lighting today, some of which is of mid-century style. (Blitzer; Lightolier)

Lloyd Manufacturing Co. United States

Lloyd Manufacturing in Menominee, Michigan, is best known for its tubular steel furniture designed by Kem Weber in the 1930s. It began in 1900 when Marshall B. Lloyd purchased a manufacturing company in Minneapolis and introduced baby carriages of hand woven reed, and furniture. In 1907 he moved to Menominee, and together with Lewis Larsen, patented a method for making metal tubing by rolling flat steel and welding it. They became the exclusive supplier of windshield frame tubing for the Ford Model T. They also introduced power looms which made the company one of the largest producers of baby carriages. In 1921 the company was acquired by Heywood-Wakefield, and they continued to produce baby carriages and children's toys until the 1930s, when they made tubular steel furniture designed by Alfons Bach and Kem Weber. (Rouland 14, 41)

Bruno Mathsson (1907-1988) Sweden

Bruno Mathsson was born in Värnamo, Sweden, and was trained as a cabinetmaker by his father Karl Mathsson from 1923 through 1931. In 1933 he began designing furniture for his father's company and then for the firm of Dux Mobel. He developed new ways for bending and laminating using industrial processes and although his focus was on architecture from 1945 to 1958, he became a leading figure in the development of Scandinavian Modern furniture.

International recognition included the 1937 Paris Exhibition of Modern Applied Arts; the Gregor Paulsson Medal in Stockholm in 1955; furniture designs exhibited in Stockholm in 1963, Oslo in 1976, Dresden in 1976, and New York in 1982. His Eva chair of bent plywood, solid birch, and hemp webbing was made by the firm of Karl Mathsson and then reissued by Dux, of Sweden from 1966. From 1958 on, he designed furniture in collaboration with Piet Hein. (Fiell, *Chairs*; Zahle 284)

Roberto Sebastian Matta (b. 1911) Chile

Roberto Sebastian Matta was born in Santiago and studied at Catholic University in Chile and received a degree in architecture from the University of Chile in 1931. He worked in the office of Le Corbusier in Paris. In 1937 he met René Magritte, Joan Miró, and Pablo

Picasso; he exhibited in 1938. The next year Matta left for New York, and in 1940 had a one-man show at the Julien Levy Gallery. He returned to Paris in 1948, and in the late 1950s turned more to sculpture. During the 1960s and 1970s he was politically active against the junta in Chile. His sculptural Malitte seating system, comprised of blocks of polyurethane foam covered with upholstery, was produced by Gavina in Italy 1966-1968 and then by Knoll International 1968-1974. (Fiell, *Chairs*; Pile 167)

Paul McCobb (1917-1969) United States

Rather than a background in art or architecture, Paul McCobb had experience selling furniture and creating displays. In 1945 he formed his own company to produce reasonably priced furniture aimed at the young market. His 1949 Planner Group of modular furniture made of hard birch was produced by the Winchedon Furniture Co. in Winchedon, Massachusetts, and was a great success. It included a platform bench after the classic Nelson design; in 1952 he introduced wrought iron bases to the group. Alternative bases, hardware, and finishes provided choices while maintaining economical manufacture. The Irwin Collection for Calvin Furniture of Grand Rapids, Michigan, was also designed in 1952. This included the use of brass in the overall structure, and included a

Paul McCobb metal label.

room divider of polished brass and mahogany. The series also offered tops of white vitrolite glass or marble. The Calvin Group for Calvin Furniture was introduced in 1954 with solid brass square tubing, mahogany, and leather on some pieces.

Other McCobb furniture groups include Directional, Predictor, Linear, and Perimeter, and additional McCobb designs were for wrought iron dining groups, plant stands, and chaises made by Arbuck in Brooklyn, New York; the chaise won a Good Design Award from the Museum of Modern Art in 1953. A walnut frame armchair was made by Meyer-Gunther-Martini in New York; in the late 1950s he developed a system of mass produced modular cabinet and counter components for the Mutschler Co.; and he also designed ceramic accessories for Phil Cutler of New York. (Hiesinger 361; Pile 168; SID)

Ludwig Mies van der Rohe (1886-1969) Germany

A leading proponent of International Style, Ludwig Mies van der Rohe is also significant to mid-century design for his influence and for the reissue of earlier designs which have come to symbolize both Bauhaus and later modernism. Born in Aachen, Germany and trained as a builder, he moved to Berlin in 1905 to study under Bruno Paul. He practiced architecture in the office of Peter Behrens from 1908 through 1911. From 1921 he was a member of the Deutscher Werkbund and became vice-president in 1926. He organized the Stuttgart Exhibition of 1927 and designed the German Pavilion for the 1929 Barcelona International Exhibition and

Mies van der Rohe Barcelona chairs, made practically all by hand.

Mies couch.

the classic Barcelona chair, which was reissued by Knoll Associates in 1948. From 1929 through 1930 he designed the Tugendhat house in Brno, Czechoslovakia along with the Brno and Tugendhat chairs. In 1930 he served as the last director of the Bauhaus and in 1938 emigrated to the United States and taught at the Illinois Institute of Technology in Chicago. Among his furniture designs reissued by Knoll are the MR chair of 1927, MR lounges of 1931, Brno chair of 1929, Barcelona chair and stool of 1929, and the Tugendhat chair, couch, and table of 1930. (Gandy; Knoll; MOMA; Stimpson)

George Nakashima (1905-1990) Japan; United States

Born in Washington state, George Nakashima studied at L'Ecole Fontainebleau outside Paris, earned a B.A. in Architecture from the University of Washington, and a Masters degree in architecture from MIT in 1930. He spent the 1930s abroad, mostly in Japan, and worked for Antonin Raymond's architectural firm from 1937 through 1939. When he returned to Seattle in 1940, he married Marion Okajiima and then established his first furniture shop in 1941. He moved to New Hope, Pennsylvania, in 1946 and established a new shop. After meeting Hans Knoll, Nakashima agreed to design furniture for mass production; in 1957 he also de-

signed a line for Widdicomb-Mueller. The American Institute of Architects awarded him a Craftsmanship Medal in 1952; in 1962 he won a National Gold Medal, Exhibition of Building Arts; in 1979 Nakashima became a Fellow of the American Craft Council; in 1981 he won the Hazlett Award for Crafts. Nakashima is a philosopher, a writer, an architect, a craftsman, and a designer of furniture. He has been appropriately called the "elder statesman of the American craft movement." (Ostergard *Full* 17-20)

George Nelson (1908-1986) United States

One of the great designers of the twentieth century, George Nelson was born in Hartford, Connecticut, in 1908. His father Simeon came to the United States from Russia at age fifteen and later became a pharmacist with his own drug store. His mother Lilian Canterow Nelson was born in the United States; both her parents were physicians. In 1924, at the age of sixteen, Nelson entered Yale University to study architecture and graduated in 1928; he also earned a Bachelor of Fine Arts degree from Yale in 1931 and did graduate work at Catholic University in Washington D. C. From 1932 to 1934 he went to graduate school on fellowship at the American Academy in Rome and was awarded the Prix de Rome for architecture. More interested in writing about than practicing architecture, he joined the staff of *Architectural Forum* as associate editor and then co-managing editor from 1935 to 1944. During those years, he also developed his career as an industrial designer, became a registered architect in the state of New York, and joined the faculty at Yale. Nelson was design director of Herman Miller from 1946 to 1972 and then remained as a consultant designer until he died in 1986. While designing for Herman Miller, Nelson also ran his own design firm, Nelson & Associates (and variations of the name) which he formed in 1947 in partnership with Gordon Chadwick. His first marriage to Frances Hollister in 1933 ended in divorce, and in 1960 he married Jacqueline Wilkenson; he had three sons.

The list of Nelson's accomplishments (see Abercrombie) is astounding — from publications on design and design philosophy, to furniture that would help form the definition of modernism. His first Herman Miller collection in 1946, totaling about eighty pieces, was a collaboration with Irving Harper and Ernest Farmer. Important designs include Herman Miller Basic Storage Components, 1946; Comprehensive Storage System, 1958; Action Office System with Bob Probst, 1965; numerous classics such as Marshmallow Sofa, 1952, Coconut Chair, 1956, Kangaroo Chair, 1956, Catenary group, 1963, and Sling sofa, which was added to the perma-

Nelson Pretzel chair. *Photo courtesy Herman Miller.*

nent collection of the Museum of Modern Art in 1964. In addition to furniture, Nelson designed the 1949 collection of Modern Clocks and the Bubble lamps for Howard Miller, Herman Miller showrooms, graphics, textiles, dinnerware, glassware, and interiors. Awards include 1953 Best Office of the Year from the *New York Times*; Gold Medal, Art Directors Club of New York; 1954 Good Design award, Museum of Modern Art; Product Design Award, Milan Triennale; 1954 Trailblazer Award for Furniture Design, National Home Furnishings League; and numerous other awards for design excellence until he died in 1986. (Abercrombie)

Nelson Marshmallow sofa, 1956. *Photo Rooks Studio, courtesy Herman Miller.*

Nessen Studios United States

Greta von Nessen (1900-c. 1978) and Walter von Nessen, trained in Bauhaus design in Germany (d. 1942), and founded Nessen Studios in New York in 1927. They specialized in the design and production of modern lamps, such as the classic double swing arm table lamps designed by Walter. After Walter died, Greta continued to operate the firm and designed and produced the Anywhere lamp in 1952. This versatile lamp could be hung, wall-mounted, or set on a table, and it was in the Good Design Exhibit at the Metropolitan Museum of Art in the same year. (Pile 186)

Isamu Noguchi (1904-1988) United States

Isamu Noguchi was born in Los Angeles but lived in Japan until 1918. He returned to the United States and studied medicine and then sculpture in New York. He was awarded a Guggenheim Fellowship and studied with Constantin Brancusi in Paris from 1927 through 1928. Noguchi returned to the United States in 1931, and his major sculpture commissions were often associated with architecture.

His first furniture design was in 1939 for a rosewood and glass table in the Biomorphic style for Conger Goodyear, president of the Museum of Modern Art. Noguchi was recruited by Herman Miller and designed a similar table with a freeform sculptural base and biomorphic glass top in 1947. In 1954 he designed a chromed steel Rocking stool and other pieces for Knoll, as well as furniture for Alcoa. Lamp design was another mid-century interest, and in 1948 he designed a simple three-legged cylinder lamp for Knoll. This led to his series of Akari lights made in Japan. These paper spheres, sculptural versions of traditional Japanese paper lamps, were produced for 25 years. (Eidelberg 389; Fehrman 46-51; Julier 145)

Verner Panton (b. 1926) Denmark; Switzerland

Trained at the Odense Technical School and the Royal Danish Academy of Fine Arts in Copenhagen, Verner Panton joined Arne Jacobsen's architectural practice (1950-1952). In 1955 he opened his own design office in Bissingen, Switzerland and is credited with designing the first single-form injection-molded plastic chair. He designed for Thonet and for Herman Miller in steel wire, molded plywood and plastic. His single-form plastic Stacking chair of 1960 through 1967 was also produced by Herman Miller from 1968 to 1979 and is in the permanent collection of the Museum of Modern Art. Panton's upholstered Cone chair was made from 1958-c. 1966; the Wire Cone chair from 1959; Pantonova Wire furniture from 1961

Panton Cone chair.

Paulin design.

to 1966; and the Panton System 1-2-3, consisting of freeform sculptural chairs with three different seat heights, in 1974. He also designed lighting, textiles, and carpets, and he won the Interior Design Award in 1963 and 1968 in the United States, and the Diploma of Honor at the International Furniture Exhibition in 1969 in Vienna. (Fehrman 82; Fiell, *Chairs*; Stimpson 106-7)

Pierre Paulin (b. 1927) France

Pierre Paulin studied sculpture at L'Ecole Camondo and graduated from L'Ecole Nationale Supérieure des Arts Décoratifs in Paris. He designed furniture for Thonet in 1954 and for Artifort from 1958. His work is fluid and sculptural and stresses comfort and ergonomics. In the mid-1960s he designed upholstered foam chairs for Artifort; his Chair 577 called both

Warren Platner wire lounge chairs with natural woven upholstery and matching side table with marble top.
Photo courtesy Skinner, Inc.

Birds in Flight and Tongue chair, is in the permanent collection of the Museum of Modern Art in New York and in the Musée des Arts Décoratifs in Paris. In 1968 he was commissioned to refurbish the Louvre; in 1969 he won an American Industrial Design Award for the Ribbon Chair, and he has won gold medals at the Brussels International Exposition and at Milan Trienales. In 1970 he designed seating for Expo '70 in Osaka, Japan; in 1975 he founded ADSA and Partners. In addition to furniture, Paulin has designed telephones, packaging, and interiors. (Fiell, *Chairs*; Pile 198; Stimpson 148-9)

Warren Platner (b. 1919) United States

"It is important that if you design a chair you produce something which enhances the person in it, because the basic premise in the first place is ridiculous from a visual standpoint. I think that's why chairs are so difficult to design. Buildings are easy." (Platner quoted in Larrabee 157)

Warren Platner was born in Baltimore. He studied at the School of Architecture at Cornell University and graduated in 1941. From 1945 to 1950 he worked in the design office of Raymond Loewy and the architectural firms of I.M. Pei and Keven Roche & John Dinkeloo. Beginning in 1960, Platner worked for Eero Saarinen and Associates in Birmingham Hills, Michigan, until 1965 when he began his own firm, Platner Associates, in New Haven, Connecticut, with emphasis on architecture. Between 1953 and 1967 Platner worked on a group of chairs and tables under a Graham Foundation grant. The designs are based on a cage-like structure of curved wires welded together. His most noted furniture design is the Platner Collection of nickel-plated steel wire furniture for Knoll in 1966, which is still being produced. (Fiell, *Chairs*; Larrabee 157; Pile 204-5)

Gio Ponti (1897-1979) Italy

Born in Milan, Gio Ponti studied architecture at the Milan Polytechnic and graduated in 1921. A major modernist designer in Italy, Ponti designed ceramics for Richard Ginori, architecture, stage sets, interiors, appliances, lighting, metalware, textiles, and furniture. In 1928 he founded the important design journal *Domus* and became its first editor; *Stile* was founded in 1941. His multi-faceted career included directing the Monza Biennale from 1925 to 1979, collaborating in the development of the Milan Triennale Exhibitions and the Compasso D'Oro award programs, teaching architecture at the Milan Polytechnic from 1936 to 1961, designing ocean liner interiors such as the Conte Grande and the Andrea Doria in 1950, and contributing regularly to *Domus* and to *Casabella*. In the 1950s he collaborated with Piero Fornasetti to design furniture and interiors. Ponti designed the classic Superleggera chair (1955-1957), which has been produced by Cassina from 1957 to the present. Other companies that have produced his designs include Altamira, Artflex, Arredoluce, and Nordiska Kompaniet. Ponti also wrote nine books and about 300 articles. (Fiell, *Chairs*; Hiesinger 373-4; Pile 207)

Ernest Race (1913-1964) England

    Ernest Race was born in Newcastle-upon-Tyne. He studied at the Bartlett School of Architecture in London from 1932 through 1935 and then worked as a draftsman for Troughton & Young Lighting Co., which made very modern Bauhaus-type lighting. In 1937 he visited his missionary aunt, who managed a weaving village in Madras, India. When Race returned to London, he incorporated his own modern abstract patterns onto the Indian textiles and sold them through his shop. Numerous architects, such as Walter Gropius, used the textiles.

    Due to shortages of materials during the war, most British furniture design and manufacture was controlled by the Board of Trade and called Utility Furniture. Race's involvement with the design and production of this economical furniture lead to the founding of Ernest Race

Inc. in partnership with Noel Jordan in 1945. Jordan, an engineer, became managing director, and Race was director and chief designer for the mass production of inexpensive high-quality contemporary furniture. Race's Antelope chair and table, produced from 1950 on, was shown at the Festival of Britain in 1951 and won a silver medal at the 1954 Milan Triennale. His cast aluminum alloy BA chair was shown at the "Britain Can Make It" exhibit at the Victoria and Albert Museum in 1946, and it won a gold medal at the 1954 Milan Triennale. In 1953 Race was made a Royal Designer for Industry. His Neptune deck chair of 1953 marked the company's entry into the contract furniture industry, followed by the Mermaid steamer chair in 1953 and the award winning Cormorant folding outdoor chair in 1959. (Conway)

Jens Risom (b. 1916) Denmark; United States

    Originally from Copenhagen, Jens Risom studied at the School for Art and Applied Design in Copenhagen from 1935 through 1938. He then emigrated to the United States in 1939 and worked for Dan Cooper Studio designing textiles and interiors. He met Hans Knoll (who was one year older to the day), and along with their wives, they traveled around the United States for four months talking to architects and designers. Risom joined Knoll and designed his

Fig. 2

Fig. 1

JENS RISOM.
INVENTOR.

BY

Malue & Spam
AT. Y

United States Patent Office drawing of chair designed by Jens Risom for Knoll, filed Sept. 18, 1943.

first furniture line in 1942. The first item was a simple straight chair made with surplus Army webbing, which inspired about fifteen pieces in the line and brought Knoll into the modern furniture business. Risom also designed the first Knoll showroom. The two collaborated on other projects, such as interiors for the General Motors Pavilion press lounge and a modern kitchen in the "America at Home" exhibit of the New York World's Fair. After serving in the United States army, in 1947 he began Jens Risom Design Inc. and ended the relationship with Knoll. He ran his design business until 1971 when it was sold to Dictaphone, and Risom stayed on as chief executive until he headed a free-lance design service called Design Control, in New Haven, Connecticut. Risom won the Brooklyn Museum Modernism Design Award for Lifetime Achievement. (Jesperson; Larrabee 41; Pulos 83-5)

Terrance Harold (T. H.) Robsjohn-Gibbings (1905-1976) England

T. H. Robsjohn-Gibbings was born in London and studied architecture at the University of Liverpool and London University. He worked as a designer and a film art director in London, worked in New York from 1929, returned to London in 1933, and in 1936 moved to New York and opened a showroom on Madison Ave.

His interior design combined modernism and classicism with the opulence of the decorating trade. He designed furniture for the John Widdicomb Co. from 1943 to 1956, including a biomorphic glass-topped coffee table in the manner of Noguchi's model for Herman Miller. In 1960 he designed a line of classic Greek furniture that was produced by Saridis in Athens, and a Klismos chair of walnut and woven leather in 1961, also for Saridis, which is at the Cooper-Hewitt Museum. After settling in Athens in 1964, he designed for clients such as Aristotle Onassis. An author as well as a designer, Robsjohn-Gibbings wrote *Goodbye Mr. Chippendale* in 1944, a spoof on American interior decorating; *Mona Lisa's Mustache* in 1947, poking fun at modern art; and *Homes of the Brave* in 1954, which poked fun at both extremes of traditional and modern decorating. (Byars 476; Pile 223)

Gilbert Rohde (1894-1994) United States

Born in New York City, Gilbert Rohde learned cabinetmaking at his father's shop. He is considered a pioneer industrial designer and key figure in the introduction of modern design in the United States. In 1923 he worked full time as a furniture illustrator for Abraham & Strauss department store in New York. After traveling in Europe (he married Gladys Vorsanger in Paris) and becoming acquainted with the Bauhaus, he opened an industrial design office in New York and produced his own furniture.

Rohde is particularly important for introducing modern design at Herman Miller, which started the company in a totally new direction beginning in 1930. To his credit are modular units, sectional sofas, storage units, the company's first metal furniture, and a variety of seating pieces. He also brought Herman Miller into the office furniture business with his Executive Office Group (EOG) in which fifteen pieces combined to make 400 groupings. He also designed furniture for John Widdicomb, Thonet, Brown-Saltzman, Kroehler, Lloyd, Valentine Seaver, Valley Upholstery, the Z stools and other chromed metal furniture for Troy Sunshade in Troy, Ohio, in the 1930s, and a line of indoor-outdoor furniture for Heywood-Wakefield in 1930. Other items included clocks for Howard Miller, water coolers, boilers, pianos, stokers, and gas ranges; exhibits included the "Design For Living" house at the 1933 Chicago World's Fair, Texas Centennial, San Francisco Golden Gate Exhibition, and several installations at the 1939 New York World's Fair. He headed the industrial design program at the New York School of Architecture from 1939 to 1943. (Ostergard & Hanks; Pulos)

Gilbert Rohde dining room set in 1934 installation. *Photo courtesy Herman Miller.*

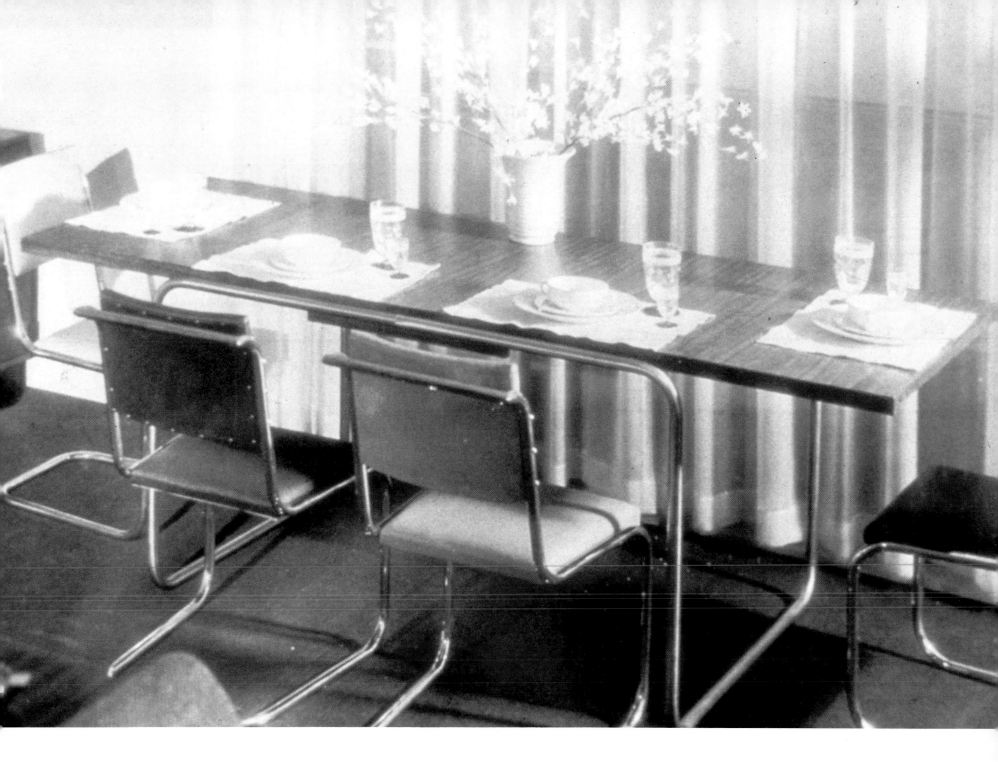

Rohde bedroom set in 1939 installation. *Photo courtesy Herman Miller.*

Eero Saarinen (1910-1961) Finland; United States

Son of famous Finnish architect and designer Eliel Saarinen, Eero was born in Kirkkonummi, Finland, and came to the United States in 1923. He studied sculpture in Paris and then earned a B. F. A. in Architecture from Yale in 1934. He returned to Finland in 1934 and worked for Karl Eklund in Helsinki until 1936, when he joined his father's architectural firm. Saarinen opened his own firm and had many major architectural commissions of colleges, airports, and public buildings, such as the Smithsonian Institute Art Gallery, Dulles International Airport Terminal Building, IBM Corp. in Rochester, Minnesota, and in Yorktown, New York, the University of Michigan Master Plan, and CBS headquarters in New York City.

His furniture was designed to be sculptural, comfortable, and economical, and was already shown in 1940 with Charles Eames at the Museum of Modern Art Organic Design Furniture competition and won two first prizes. His designs for Knoll Associates include the Plywood chair in 1946, Womb chair in 1946, Grasshopper chair in the late 1940s, and Pedestal furniture in 1958. Saarinen married Lily Swann in 1939, divorced, and married Aline Louchheim in 1953 and had three children, Eric, Susan, and Eames. He was honored with many awards, such as a Gold Medal from the American Institute of Architects (AIA), and was an AIA Fellow. He taught at Cranbrook, where the Saarinen house stands and can be toured by the public. (Saarinen 104-5; Detroit 273)

Grasshopper chair, the first design by Eero Saarinen for Knoll Associates, in the late 1940s, bent birch arms and legs. *Photo courtesy Treadway Gallery.*

Count Alexis de Sakhnoffsky

Alexis de Sakhnoffsky came to the United States in the 1920s and established a reputation for his use of streamlined design. A prominent stylist of custom automobiles in the 1920s and 1930s, such as Cord, Auburn, and Studebaker, he incorporated speed and movement into other designs as well. He was an artist and contributor to *Esquire* magazine, wrote and published drawings on streamlining, and designed tricycles and pedal cars for Steelcraft in 1937. His contribution to furniture design was at Heywood-Wakefield, where he designed the classic kneehole desk with wood drawer handles shaped like airplane wings and other items for their Modern line. (Rouland)

Carlo Scarpa (1906-1978) Italy

Born in Venice, Italy, Carlo Scarpa studied architecture at Accademia di Bella Arte in Venice until 1926. He is known for his glass designs for Venini from 1933 to 1977, but he also designed silver, furniture, and interiors. He designed exhibits and pavilions at the Venice Biennales and Milan Triennales and an exhibit of Frank Lloyd Wright designs in Milan in 1960. Renowned for his interior design, such as the Olivetti showroom in Venice, he was also responsible for important renovations, notably the Venice Academy in 1952, the National Gallery

Detail of Sakhnoffsky design for Heywood-Wakefield.

of Sicily from 1953 to 1954, and six rooms of the Uffizi. Scarpa taught at the Venice Art Institute from 1945 through 1947, directed the Institute of Architecture at the University of Venice from 1972 to 1978, and was elected Honorary

Royal Designer for Industry, London. His Bastiano upholstery system for Knoll consisted of simple rectangular furniture after Wright. His son Tobia Scarpa (b. 1935) also designed furniture for Knoll and for Cassina, known for its soft form, including the Sirano chair for Cassina in 1968. (Byars, 498; Pile 237)

Richard Schultz (b. 1926) United States

Richard Schultz studied at Iowa State University, the Illinois Institute of Technology, and the Chicago School of Design. He joined Knoll in 1951 and worked with Harry Bertoia designing a group of wire furniture in 1952. "We knew from the very beginning that these chairs were going to be extraordinary...I can remember feeling that I was working on something that was on a very high level" (Larrabee 22). Schultz got the job at Knoll by showing Florence Knoll some free-hand sketches he had done in Europe. Other Knoll designs include a small Petal table, a Stacking chair, a steel-wire chaise lounge in the early 1960s, the 1966 Leisure Collection of outdoor furniture, which won a design award from the American Institute of Interior Designers in 1977, and lounge furniture in 1981. He attributed Knoll's success to hiring designers who were trained to think creatively and for being a design company first, and then a furniture company. Schultz continues to design furniture for manufacturers such as Conde House. (Larrabee 22, 152; Pile 239)

Ben Seibel United States

Besides his work for Mikasa, Seibel designed Impromptu and Informal patterns for Iroquois China shortly after Wright designed his Iroquois Casual. Although he resided in Greenwich Village in New York City, Seibel was an important designer for the Fostoria Glass Co. in Moundsville, West Virginia, especially in the 1950s and through the 1970s. Some of his Fostoria designs include Facets, Pebble Beach, Module, centerpieces with candle holders, candy jars and boxes; Corsage Plum, Monarch lead crystal, Gourmet, York lead crystal barware and stemware, and candle bud vases. Among his other mid-century designs is a desk lamp distributed by the New York based Raymor, one of the most important distributing companies of mid-century design.

Sottsass, Ettore (b. 1917) Italy

Born in Innsbruck, Ettore Sottsass's parents were Italian; the family moved to Turin in 1928 where he studied architecture at the Polytechnic school from 1934 through 1939. After the war he practiced architecture in Turin. In 1946 Sottsass moved to Milan and organized an important international abstract art exhibit, and

in the following year showed a chair design at the Milan Triennale. During the 1950s he moved from Functionalism to Organic design using plywood, metal, and plastics, and he worked briefly for George Nelson in New York in 1956. In 1957 he collaborated with Olivetti as a consultant for designing products such as typewriters. Sottsass traveled in India in 1961 and produced ceramics. A pioneer of Postmodernism, he designed furniture for Poltronova in 1965. In 1980 he formed Sottsass Associati and in 1981 started the Memphis group, known for its design focus on popular culture and use of brilliant color. (Julier 178-80; Sparke *Italian*)

Steelcase United States

The Metal Office Furniture Co. was founded in Grand Rapids in 1912 by Peter M. Wege, and was affiliated with the Macey Co. until 1918. The Steelcase trademark was adopted in 1921. In the late 1930s they collaborated with Frank Lloyd Wright to produce furniture for the offices of S. C. Johnson & Co. (JohnsonWax) in Racine, Wisconsin. On December 1, 1954 Steelcase became the official company name because of the importance of product recognition. Also in 1954, they introduced color into otherwise drab offices with furniture in colors of the Arizona desert.

By 1970 sales passed the $100 million mark and employment topped 4,000. A new headquarters housing 1,000 office workers opened in 1983. In 1985 sales broke the $1 billion mark, and Steelcase purchased Stow Davis, also in Grand Rapids. Known as manufacturers of high quality traditional wood furniture, Stow Davis introduced several lines of modern office furniture throughout the 1950s and 1960s, some

Colorado colors by Steelcase.

using freeform shapes. Today, the Steelcase Design Partnership includes the companies Ai, Brayton, Design Tex, Details, Health Design, Metro Furniture, Stow Davis, and Vecta. Though not reissuing mid-century office designs other than the classic Wright desk and chair, there is clearly a strong Fifties influence in many of the contemporary designs of furniture offered today. (Steelcase)

Harris Strong (b. 1920) United States

Harris Strong was born in Waukesha, Wisconsin, in 1920. In 1939 he went to North Carolina State University to study ceramic and chemical engineering, spent three years in the United States Army, and then graduated in 1946. He worked for Kelby Originals in Brooklyn, New York; then Strong and Robert Krasner formed a partnership and opened the Potters of Wall Street in 1947. They sold the business to Kelby Originals, and Strong joined American Art Industries in Brooklyn and made small decorative vases. In 1958 Harris G. Strong Inc. opened in Bronx, New York, and made ceramic lamps, ashtrays, and tiles. Tiles were often made just to test glazes and were not taken very seriously, but the hand-painted tiles became so popular that Strong could hardly keep up with the demand. He set up at trade shows and concentrated selling to architects and designers; by the

Four-tile vertical panel of park scene with fountain in vivid yellows and oranges with black trees; on oiled walnut plaque, 24 x 11.

early 1960s he hired fourteen artists in order to produce the tile panels needed for hotels, residences, and other walls throughout the country. Strong had little competition for tiles in the 1950s and 1960s, but when he moved to Trenton, Maine, in 1970, he stopped making them. With twenty-five employees, Strong concentrated on other framed wall art, such as prints. They are still in business (Perrault).

Walter Dorwin Teague (1883-1960) United States

Walter Dorwin Teague was a pioneer American industrial designer who promoted the Streamlined style. Born in Decatur, Indiana, he attended evening classes at the Art Students League in New York from 1903 to 1907, did freelance drawing and sign lettering, joined the Ben Hampton Advertising Agency in 1908, and then joined the Calkins-Holden agency before starting his own office in 1911. His advertising designs included the Metropolitan Museum of Art industrial art exhibit in 1922. After going to Europe in 1926 and studying the work of Le Corbusier, he returned to his practice and focused on product designs. Teague designed cameras (notably the Baby Brownie) for Eastman Kodak from 1934 to 1941, A.B. Dick showrooms, weather instruments for Taylor Instrument Co., dinnerware for Taylor, Smith & Tay-

House of Cards by Charles and Ray Eames for Tigrett, on display at Herman Miller Pavilion furniture showroom.

Another view of House of Cards.

lor, passenger cars for the New Haven Railroad, and Texaco service stations. He was on the Board of Design for the New York World's Fair and designed exhibits for Consolidated Edison, Ford Motors, United States Steel, du Pont, National Cash Register, Eastman Kodak, and A. B. Dick. In 1944 Teague became the first president of the newly formed Society of Industrial Designers (SID). Fifties designs included pens for Scripto, cans for Schaefer Beer, and airplane interiors for Boeing's 707. He wrote the book *Design This Day: The Techniques of Order in the Machine Age* in 1940. His firm, Walter Dorwin Teague Associates continued after his death. (Eidelberg 401, Pulos)

Tigrett Enterprises United States

Entrepreneur and manufacturer John Burton Tigrett sought out, developed, and marketed innovative ideas. Rather than paying a fee for development of a product, he paid a royalty on each unit sold. The round nylon net playpen is one of their items. In 1951 Tigrett Enterprises in Jackson, Tennessee, manufactured an Eames design for a construction toy consisting of colored geometric panels called The Toy. A smaller version called The Little Toy was introduced by Tigrett in 1952 and produced until 1961. Tigrett distributed (American Playing Card printed) Eames House of Cards, two sets of 54 decorated plastic-coated cards notched for building; they were introduced in 1953 at 98 cents per pack and made until 1961. They also made Giant House of Cards, twenty 7" x 11" cards made of eight-ply cardboard, intended for adults as well as children to play with. These were manufactured by Tigrett until the company went out of business in 1961. (Pulos 330-31)

Kurt Versen (b. 1901) Sweden

Kurt Versen was born in Sweden, studied in Germany, and came to the United States in 1930. He designed and manufactured modern lighting and supplied fixtures for several installations of the 1939 New York World's Fair. Many of his classic designs of the 1940s and 1950s had goose necks and swivel joints for adjustability. Versen was one of the first designers to introduce modern design at Lightolier, and his lamps were shown in the 1951 Good Design exhibit at the Museum of Modern Art. (Blitzer; Byars 570; Pile 274)

Karl Emanuel Martin (Kem) Weber (1889-1963) Germany; United States

Born in Berlin, Kem Weber became a pioneer American industrial designer, and one of the few designers on the West Coast while most were on the East Coast in the 1920s and 1930s. While still a student, he supervised the construction of the German portion of the 1910 Brussels World's Fair, and then graduated from the School of Decorative Arts in Berlin in 1912. While helping to design the German section of the 1915 San Francisco International Exhibition, he was stranded in California at the outbreak of World War I; he stayed and became a United States citizen in 1924. Weber worked as an art director and furniture designer and then opened his own industrial design studio in Hollywood in 1927. He designed in the Streamlined style and in 1934 designed the Airline chair, made of plywood hinged together and produced by the Airline Chair Co. in Los Angeles. His use of tubular steel, for furniture manufactured by Lloyd, was considered to be flamboyant, as opposed to the austere look of the International Style used by others. Weber designed prefabricated housing as well as conventional architecture and eventually turned to exclusive use of natural materials, namely wood, brick, and fieldstone. (Eidelberg 404-5; Pulos)

Hans Wegner (b. 1914) Denmark

Hans Wegner was born in the small town of Tøndor in Denmark. At the age of thirteen he began a four year apprenticeship with a local cabinetmaker. After studying at the Danish Institute of Technology in Copenhagen and at the Copenhagen School of Arts and Crafts, he lectured at the latter school from 1938 to 1942 and taught there from 1946 to 1955. Wegner designed furniture in the architectural office of Arne Jacobsen and Erik Moeller, where he met and married Inga Helbo. In 1943 he started his own design office, and he designed furniture for Johannes Hansen and Fritz Hansen of Denmark, and his designs were also distributed by Knoll. He was a member of the Royal Association of Danish Architects, and in 1959 he was made Honorary Royal Designer for Industry by the Royal Society of Arts in London. Wegner has been represented at major international exhibitions and won the Lunning Prize in 1954, the Eckersberg medal in 1956, and the Grand Prix at the Milan Triennale in 1951 and a gold medal in 1954. Considered a major designer of Danish Modern, many museums have Wegner chairs in their collections. His first chair for mass production was the Chinese chair, made by Fritz Hansen in 1944; it was followed by others, such as the simple armchair of tapered wood form with a woven seat in 1949, called the Classic chair, and the Folding chair of 1949; the Peacock chair of 1947, based on the design of the Windsor chair, which became a symbol of Danish Modern furniture; the Valet chair in 1953, and the Bull chair and ottoman in 1960. (Fehrman 61-4; Gandy; Zahle 294-5)

Edward J. Wormley (b. 1907) United States

Born on New Years Eve in Illinois, Edward Wormley studied at the Art Institute of Chicago from 1926 to 1927. He became chief designer and director of design for Dunbar Furniture Co. from 1931 to 1941 and again in 1970 just before retiring. Although he continued his affiliation with Dunbar after the war, he operated his own firm in New York City specializing in interior design from 1945 to 1967. His many designs and clients included carpets for Alexander Smith & Sons, furniture for Drexel, cabinets for RCA, lamps for Lightolier, and textiles for Schiffer Prints. In 1951 and 1952 he won Good Design Awards for six designs at the Museum of Modern Art; he was made a Fellow of the American Institute of Decorators in 1960, and he exhibited at the Milan Triennale in 1964.

Wormley was a versatile and prolific designer of furniture responsible for an average of 100 designs annually for Dunbar, in both traditional and modern styles. Among his designs are the Riemerschmid armchair #4797 c. 1946, the "Listen to me" chaise in 1947, a classic freeform coffee table, and a 150-piece Janus line with an Arts and Crafts influence in 1957. (Cyran "Wormley"; Smith)

United States Patent Office drawing of chair designed by Frank Lloyd Wright, filed Dec. 20, 1937, (used for the Johnson Wax building.)

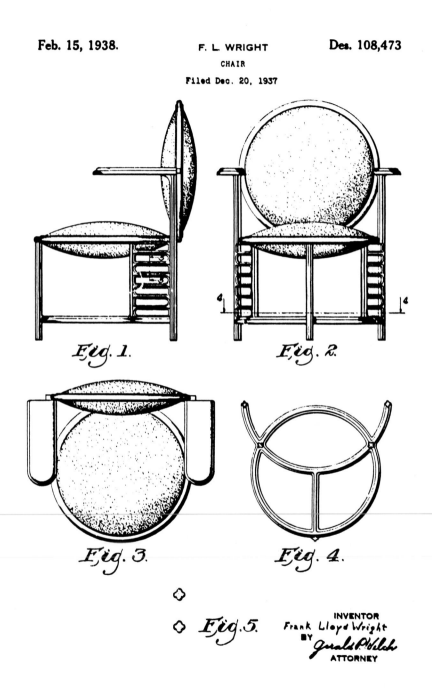

Feb. 15, 1938.   F. L. WRIGHT   Des. 108,473
CHAIR
Filed Dec. 20, 1937

Fig. 1.   Fig. 2.

Fig. 3.   Fig. 4.

Fig. 5.

INVENTOR
Frank Lloyd Wright
BY
Gerald P. Welch
ATTORNEY

Frank Lloyd Wright (1867-1959) United States

Frank Lloyd Wright is regarded as one of the most significant American architects and a pioneer modernist. He was born in Wisconsin and studied engineering at Wisconsin State University at Madison. He began by working as a draftsman for Louis Sullivan in 1887 and started his own architectural office in 1893. By 1900 Wright had designed over fifty homes and interiors. In 1895 he designed a cube chair described by his son John as the first piece of modern furniture made in the United States. Though made of wood, its lines seemed to anticipate those of the International Style, which ironically Wright was not at all associated with. He also is credited with designing the first metal office furniture, a desk with a swivel chair designed in 1904 for the Larkin Administration offices. His straight angular furniture designs in the Arts & Crafts manner were usually for individual homes rather than for mass production. In the mid-1930s, however, he designed the S. C. Johnson Wax Administration building and its unique metal desks and chairs manufactured by Steelcase (reintroduced by Cassina). In 1955 he designed the Taliesin line of furniture intended for a mass market and manufactured by Heritage Henredon Co. His Midway chair of 1914 was reintroduced by Cassina and distributed by

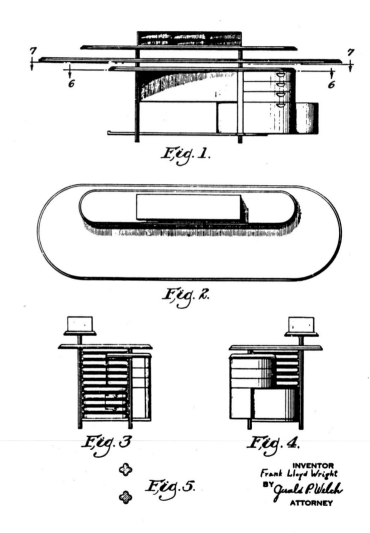

April 11, 1939.   F. L. WRIGHT   Des. 114,203
DESK
Filed Dec. 20, 1937   2 Sheets—Sheet 1

Fig. 1.

Fig. 2.

Fig. 3   Fig. 4.

Fig. 5.

INVENTOR
Frank Lloyd Wright
BY Gerald P. Welch
ATTORNEY

United States Patent Office drawings of desk designed by Frank Lloyd Wright, filed Dec. 20, 1937 (with Johnson Wax building chair)

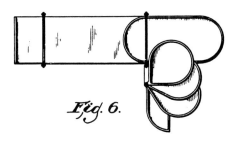

Fig. 6.

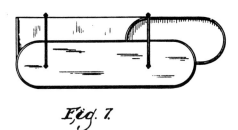

Fig. 7.

INVENTOR

Frank Lloyd Wright

BY

Gerald P Welsh

ATTORNEY

Atelier International. The hexagonal form of another chair for Midway Gardens in 1914 was his upholstered aluminum side and arm chairs designed for the Price Tower in Bartlesville, Oklahoma, c. 1953. (Garner 56-7; Heinz; Steelcase)

Russel Wright (1904-1976) United States

Born in Lebanon, Ohio, Russel Wright was a child prodigy painter, and in 1920 studied at the Cincinnati Academy of Art, the Columbia School of Architecture, and at the Art Students League in New York, where he also began designing theater costumes and sets. In 1935 he formed Russel Wright Associates with his wife Mary Einstein Wright and Irving Richards and was instrumental in bringing modern design to middle class Americans from the 1930s through the 1950s. A versatile designer, Wright became known for interior furnishings and domestic items such as the first modern blond maple furniture for Conant Ball in the 1930s and modern furniture for Heywood-Wakefield. Some of his best known designs were for pottery, especially the enormously successful American Modern dinnerware for Steubenville Pottery Co. (that sold more than 80 million pieces from 1939 to 1959), plus Iroquois Casual for Iroquois China Co., and lines for other pottery companies — Harker, Edwin M. Knowles, Paden City,

Sterling China, and Bauer Art Pottery. He designed glassware for Imperial Glass Co., Old Morgantown Glass Guild, and Fostoria Glass Co. Wright also designed melamine dinnerware, streamlined radios for Wurlitzer, toys for Ideal, metalware for Chase Brass and Copper, spun aluminum items, cocktail gadgets, pianos, chewing gum dispensers, linotype machines, packaging, fabrics, carpets, lighting fixtures, showrooms, and World's Fair exhibits. (Fehrman 65-70; Hennessey)

Sori Yanagi (b. 1915) Japan

Sori Yanagi studied painting and architecture at the Tokyo Academy of Fine Arts from 1936 to 1940. He then assisted Charlotte Perriand while she worked in Japan, until 1942. In 1952 Yanagi won a Japanese Competition for Industrial Design and also founded the Yanagi Industrial Design Institute. He taught at Tokyo Women's College of Art from 1953 to 1954 and at Kanazawa University of Arts and Crafts from 1954. He came to the United States in the 1950s. His Butterfly stool of molded plywood with a metal stretcher was designed in 1956 and represents a synthesis of Eastern and Western culture. In addition to other wooden furniture and plastic stacking stools, Yanagi also designed ceramics, metal tableware, appliances, and tractors. He became director of the Japan Folk Crafts Museum in Tokyo in 1977. (Fiell, *Chairs*; Hiesinger 399-400)

Pair of Diamond chairs designed in 1952 by Harry Bertoia for Knoll, white coated wire frame with brown and black upholstery, on black metal legs, 34" width x 28" depth x 30" height. *Photo courtesy Treadway Gallery.* $300-$400 each

Wide Diamond chair designed in 1952 by Harry Bertoia for Knoll, c. 1975, chromed wire mesh with rubber shock mounts, upholstered in rust, yellow, pale blue, and brown geometric fabric, label, 44" width x 34" depth x 28" height. *Photo courtesy Treadway Gallery.* $500-$700

Bird chair and ottoman designed by Harry Bertoia for Knoll, c. 1975, chromed wire mesh with same upholstery fabric, labels, chair 38" width x 34" depth x 39" height; ottoman 24" width x 17" depth x 14" height. *Photo courtesy Treadway Gallery.* $700-$900

Diamond chair. $300-$500

Side view of Bertoia Diamond chair with red-orange upholstery and black wire frame, 33 1/2" width x 28 1/4" depth x 30" height, 1950s, Knoll Associates label. $300-$400

Side Chair designed in 1952 by Harry Bertoia for Knoll, 21 3/4" width x 19 3/4" depth x 30" height. *Courtesy of the Cuyahoga County Public Library.*

Bertoia Diamond chair with only the seat upholstered in red-orange. *Courtesy of the Cuyahoga County Public Library.*

Child size side chair next to standard size to show relative size. *Courtesy of the Cuyahoga County Public Library.*

Above left
Group of Bertoia side chairs in use at the Beachwood Branch of the Cuyahoga County Public Library.

Group of child size Bertoia side chairs in use at the Beachwood Branch of the Cuyahoga County Public Library. $75-$150 each

Group of four Harry Bertoia wire side chairs, designed 1952, white wire finish mesh with yellow vinyl seat cushions, labels, 22" width x 29 3/4" height. *Photo courtesy Skinner, Inc.* $600-$800

Bar stools designed by Harry Bertoia for Knoll and part of the Knoll Studio Bertoia Collection. *Photo courtesy Knoll.*

Coconut chair (1955-1978) designed by George Nelson for Herman Miller, coconut wedge shaped shell of molded plastic with foam cushions, resting on a thin metal wire frame, with curved edges and chrome base, red upholstery. *Photo courtesy Herman Miller.*

Bottom, Coconut chair with black upholstery; top DAR molded fiberglass chair designed by Charles and Ray Eames for Herman Miller on display at Herman Miller Pavilion.

George Nelson Coconut chair and ottoman made by
Herman Miller, 1955-1978, with yellow upholstery on
the triangular shell; chair 40" width x 34" depth x 33"
height; ottoman 23" width x 17" depth x 14" height.
Photo courtesy Treadway Gallery. $2,000-$2,500

George Nelson Coconut ottoman, white naugahyde
upholstery, chromed steel legs. *Photo courtesy Treadway
Gallery.* $700-$900

Walnut Stools in three different profiles, designed by Charles and Ray Eames in 1960 as stools or low tables for the Time-Life Building in New York, 13 1/4" diameter x 15" height. *Photo courtesy Herman Miller.* $400-$600 each

Pair of '50s stools designed by Randall McDonald, student of Frank Lloyd Wright, with geometric bases in red metal, black vinyl upholstered seats, 15" square x 24" height. *Photo courtesy Treadway Gallery.* $300-$500

Center, reclining armchair designed by Alvar Aalto, birch frame supporting laminated bentwood seat with backrest attached with wrought iron bar, 30 3/4" width x 24 1/2" height $400-$600

Left and right, two Fan Leg, or X stools designed by Alvar Aalto for Artek, c. 1954, each leg of five laminated pieces of ash joined at the seat, leather upholstery, label, 18 1/2" width x 18" height. *Photo courtesy Skinner, Inc.* $400-$600

Far left
Pair of Z stools designed by Gilbert Rohde for the Troy Sunshade Co. in Troy, Ohio, c. 1930, red vinyl upholstery, chromed tubular steel frames, label. *Photo courtesy Skinner, Inc.* $300-$500

Left
Butterfly stool designed by Sori Yanagi in 1956, produced by Tendo Mokko, Japan, of rosewood veneered plywood with brass stretcher, labels, 16" width x 16" height. *Photo courtesy Treadway Gallery.* $900-$1,200

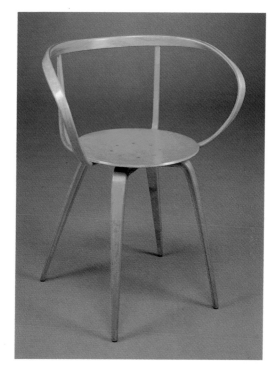

Laminated wood and metal Fin stool, Isamu Noguchi prototype, manufactured by Herman Miller, c. 1946, molded circular seat raised on a single tapering wood leg and two cylindrical metal legs. The seat for the prototype was cut out from the seat of an Eames DCW plywood chair; the final version is of thicker solid wood, produced in very limited quantities. *Photo © 1993 Sotheby's, Inc., courtesy Sotheby's New York.* $3,000-$5,000

Rare chromed steel rocking stool, which also served as a table, designed by Isamu Noguchi for Knoll, c. 1955, shaped circular seat supported by intersecting v-shaped struts on a circular rocking base. *Photo © 1993 Sotheby's, Inc., courtesy Sotheby's New York.* $2,500-$4,000

Pretzel chair designed by John Pile for George Nelson Associates in 1952, after a Thonet armchair model c. 1904, and made by Plycraft in Massachusetts for Herman Miller, of laminated wood circular seat, tapered legs, bent laminated rail forming back and arms, produced in limited quantities, and recreated in 1957 by Paul Goldman, president of Plycraft. *Photo ©1993 Sotheby's, Inc., courtesy Sotheby's New York.* $1,800-$2,200

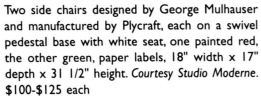

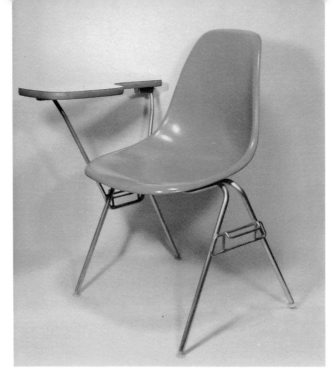

Two side chairs designed by George Mulhauser and manufactured by Plycraft, each on a swivel pedestal base with white seat, one painted red, the other green, paper labels, 18" width x 17" depth x 31 1/2" height. *Courtesy Studio Moderne.* $100-$125 each

School desk-chair in turquoise molded fiberglass, designed by Charles and Ray Eames in 1964 for Herman Miller, a modification of the early 1950s stacking chair, with folding white laminate tablet, metal legs, label. $75-$125

Stack of Eames school desk-chairs, ideal for buffet serving.

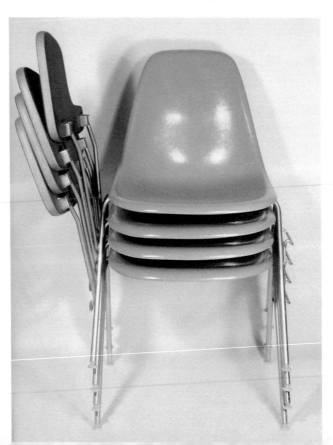

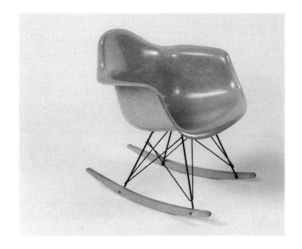

Left, DAR armchair designed by Charles and Ray Eames for Herman Miller, c. 1949, blue molded fiberglass seat, steel rod base, label; right similar DAR swivel armchair, c. 1949, with gray seat on swivel base with wooden legs and black finished steel struts, label. *Photo courtesy Skinner, Inc.* $200-$300; $500-$700

Upper left
Zenith rocker designed by Charles and Ray Eames for Herman Miller, c. 1951, long tapering birch runners, black metal struts, label, 25" width x 26" depth x 27" height. *Photo courtesy Treadway Gallery.* $400-$600

Eames molded fiberglass chair on Eiffel Tower base. *Photo Rooks Studio, courtesy Herman Miller.* $200-$300

Seating 83

Saarinen Tulip or Pedestal armchair introduced in 1956
by Knoll, white molded fiberglass shell with red cushion, on white pedestal base, 26" width x 23 1/2" depth
x 32" height, in the Knoll Studio Saarinen Collection.
Photo courtesy Knoll.

Set of four DCM (Dining Chair Metal) chairs designed by Charles and Ray Eames and introduced by Herman Miller in 1946, 5-ply molded plywood seats and backs, chromed metal frames, each 20 1/2" width x 20 1/2" depth x 29 1/2" height. *Photo courtesy Treadway Gallery.* $100-$200 each

Eames LCM (Lounge Chair Metal) and DCM molded plywood chairs. *Photo courtesy Herman Miller.* $150-$250; $100-$200

LCW (Lounge Chair Wood) molded plywood chair designed by Charles and Ray Eames for Herman Miller, originally produced from 1946 to 1957, black ebony finish, 22" width x 22" depth x 26 1/2" height, reissued herman miller for the home 1994, on display at Herman Miller Pavilion.

LCW molded plywood chair by Charles and Ray Eames, back and seat covered in cow skin. *Photo courtesy Treadway Gallery.* $600-$800

Three LCW chairs in original natural finish, 1946-1957. *Photo courtesy Skinner, Inc.* $400-$600 each

LCM molded plywood chair. *Photo Charles Eames, courtesy Herman Miller.*

Three Hans Wegner style chairs, each made in Denmark with laminated bentwood back on maple frame, black and white upholstered seat, 21 1/2" width x 29 1/4" height. *Photo courtesy Skinner, Inc.* $150-$200 each

Four Gio Ponti Superleggera (super light) style chairs, each of woven vinyl-coated rope seat in black and white, chromed steel frame, made by Cassina from 1957, "Made in Italy" decal, 16 1/4" width x 32" height. *Photo courtesy Skinner, Inc.* $100-$200 each

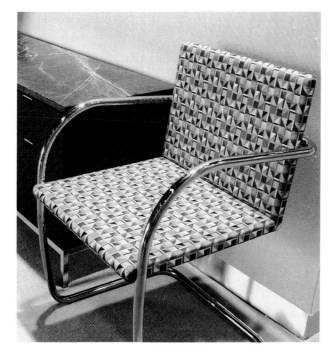

Brno flat bar stainless steel chair with arm pads, originally designed in 1929 by Mies van der Rohe for his house in Brno, Czechoslovakia, and one of four models of the Knoll Studio Brno Chair. *Photo courtesy Knoll.*

Brno chair of tubular stainless steel with leather upholstery, another version of the original Brno chair, part of the Knoll Studio Mies van der Rohe Collection. *Photo courtesy Knoll.*

Tubular steel Brno chair with geometric upholstered seat, on display at Knoll in Grand Rapids.

Three MR chairs after a design by Ludwig Mies van der
Rohe, c. 1929, chromed tubular steel frame, split cane
seat and wrapping, 20 1/2" width x 31 1/2" height. *Photo
Courtesy Skinner, Inc.* $100-$200 each

Pair of Matteo Grassi chromed metal armchairs with
black leather upholstery, 24" width x 31 1/2" height.
Photo courtesy Skinner, Inc. $150-$250 each

Left, pair of armchairs designed by Eero Saarinen for Knoll Associates in 1957, blue upholstered seats on tubular steel legs, 25 3/8" width x 31 1/2" height, labels. $300-$500 each

Right, pair of Stendig chromed and lacquered armchairs with yellow upholstered seats and backs, made in Finland, label, 23 1/2" width x 29 1/4" height. *Photo courtesy of Skinner, Inc.* $200-$300 each

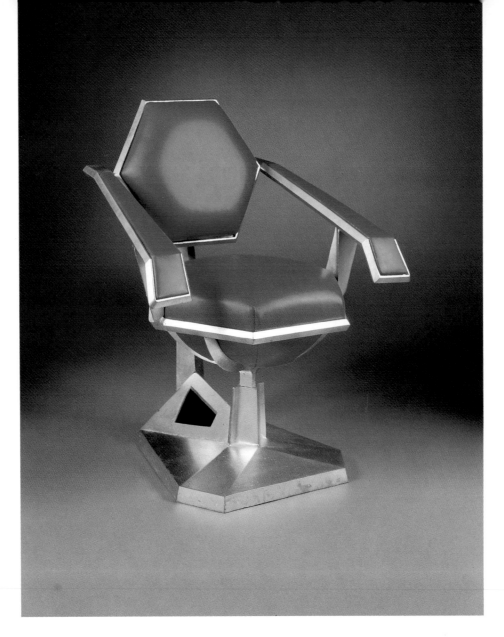

Frank Lloyd Wright upholstered aluminum armchair, designed for the Price Tower, Bartlesville, Oklahoma, c. 1953, the hexagonal swivelling back flanked by sloping shaped arms above a hexagonal seat, raised on a molded platform base, the aluminum frame painted silver, red leather upholstery, an identical model in the collection of the Metropolitan Museum of Art. The form is reminiscent of Wright's hexagonal Art Deco designs for Midway Gardens c. 1914 and the Imperial Hotel in Tokyo c. 1920. *Photo ©1993 Sotheby's, Inc., courtesy Sotheby's New York.* $10,000-$12,000

Brushed aluminum armchair upholstered in red-orange vinyl, chair back moves freely with flexible attachment to seat, made by General Fireproofing, Youngstown, Ohio, 22 1/4" width x 20 3/4" depth x 31 1/2" height, label. $100-$150

Warren Platner wire lounge chair with oatmeal velour upholstery on wire rod base, label, 36" width x 26" depth x 30" height. *Photo courtesy Treadway Gallery.* $400-$600

Seating 93

Pair of Warren Platner wire chairs, orange upholstery on black-finished wire bases and wire backs, labels. *Photo courtesy Skinner, Inc.* $500-$700 each

Pair of caned walnut and black steel armchairs by George Nelson for Herman Miller, the rectangular caned back joined to wooden armrests by geometric black finished steel frame, supporting wide squared seat, upholstered in orange, green, and purple striped fabric, 33" height. *Photo courtesy Christie's New York.* $200-$300 each

Pair of Mushroom chairs designed by Eero Aarnio for Stendig in 1965, hand woven bleached wicker on rattan frame, decal label, 32" diameter x 26" height. *Photo courtesy Skinner, Inc.* $250-$350 each

Chieftain armchair designed by Finn Juhl in 1949, produced by Niels Vodder, Denmark, teak frame with leather upholstery, label, 35" width x 40" depth x 36 3/4" height. *Photo courtesy Skinner, Inc.* $1,000-$1,500

Scandinavian Modern walnut folding chair, organic design frame with adjustable seat, tacked leather sling seat and back upholstery, folding contoured arms, 23" width x 36" height. *Photo courtesy Skinner, Inc.* $400-$500

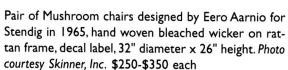

Four Danish Modern armchairs, curved wood back with five spindles, woven rope seats, stamped "Made in Denmark," 22" width x 29 1/2" height. *Photo courtesy Skinner, Inc.* $100-$150 each

Four armchairs designed by Eero Saarinen for Knoll Associates in 1948, laminated bent birch legs, gray upholstery, labels, 22" width x 30 3/4" height; with Jens Risom coffee table with mahogany legs and laminate top, paper label, 32" length x 23 1/2" width x 13 1/2" height. *Photo courtesy Skinner, Inc.* $200-$250 each, $300-$400

96 Fifties Furniture

Six Heywood Wakefield dining chairs, one armchair and five side chairs, in birch with bow tie backs and upholstered seats, 17" width x 16" depth x 31" height. *Photo courtesy of Treadway Gallery.* $100-$125 each

Heywood-Wakefield rattan lounge chair with original upholstery. *Courtesy Studio Moderne.* $200-$300

Seating 97

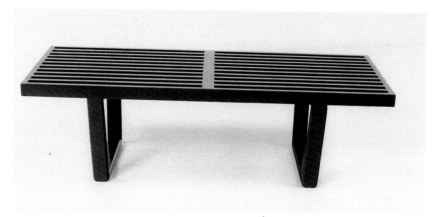

Nelson Platform bench made by Herman Miller, black ebonized two-section top and two legs, 48" width x 18 1/2" depth x 14 1/2" height. *Photo courtesy Treadway Gallery.* $500-$700

Nelson Platform bench showing three sections and two legs. *Photo courtesy of Treadway Gallery.* $700-$900

The Platform bench (1946-1967) was originally called a Slat bench until 1961, when the Black Frame Group was introduced. It was a wood bench with a slatted top that rested on trapezoid-shaped frames of either light or ebonized wood. The shape of the Platform bench was unique to these pieces and different from the Black Frame bench. Platform benches often appeared with basic cabinet series cases which rested atop. Dimensions were 24" high x 18 1/2" deep. Widths varied according to year of manufacture: widths in 1946 were 48", 68", 72", and 102"; widths of 56 3/16" and 92" were added in 1949. Bench tops came in both natural birch or ebonized wood. Bases had the same options, plus satin chrome or black metal legs. (Herman Miller Archives) The Platform bench has been reintroduced in "herman miller for the home."

Nelson Platform bench made by Herman Miller 1946-1967, blond wood four-section top with three ebonized wood legs, 102" width x 18" depth x 14" height. *Photo courtesy Treadway Gallery.* $1,000-$1,500

George Nakashima sofa with spindle back in solid walnut, open arms, six tapered rounded legs, recent mustard yellow upholstery, 74" width x 27" depth x 30" height. *Photo courtesy Treadway Gallery.* $2,000-$2,500

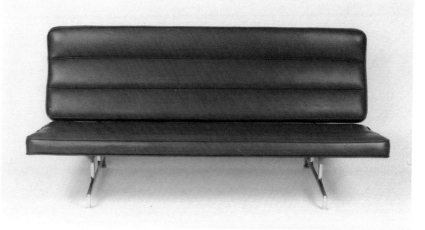

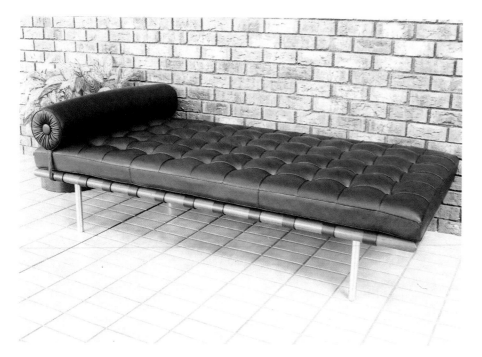

Sofa 3473 designed by Charles and Ray Eames for Herman Miller (1964-1973), three horizontal section seat and back, upholstered in bright blue naugahyde, on polished aluminum base, tag, 72" width x 30" depth x 33" height. *Photo courtesy Treadway Gallery.* $1,000-$1,500

Upper left
Compact sofa (Sofa Compact) designed in 1954 by Charles and Ray Eames for Herman Miller, the last piece of "low-cost" furniture attempted by the office, two panel back and seat in charcoal naugahyde, chromed base, label, 72 1/2" width x 30" depth x 35" height. *Photo courtesy Treadway Gallery.* $900-$1,200

Couch designed by Mies van der Rohe in 1930, and the first piece by Mies to combine wood and metal, later produced by Knoll, this example from the Knoll Studio Mies van der Rohe Collection, on display at Knoll in Grand Rapids, 78" length x 39" width x 15 1/2" height.

Pair of Barcelona chairs designed by Mies van der Rohe for Knoll Associates in 1929, almost entirely made by hand, stainless steel X-frame with red straps and red welted leather upholstery, in the Knoll Studio Mies van der Rohe Collection, on display at Knoll, in Grand Rapids.

Pair of Barcelona chairs designed by Mies van der Rohe for Knoll Associates, stainless steel X-frame with brown leather straps and brown suede upholstery, labels, 30" square x 29" height. *Photo courtesy Treadway Gallery.* $1,200-$1,800 each

Barcelona stool designed by Mies van der Rohe in 1929, tan leather upholstery, chromed steel legs, label, 23 1/2" width x 22" depth x 14 1/2" height. *Photo courtesy Skinner, Inc.* $1,000-$1,500

Three-seat sofa, c. 1930s, streamlined style tubular chromed metal frame, reupholstered in maroon and gray fabric, 68" width x 36" depth x 29" height. *Photo courtesy Treadway Gallery.* $600-$800

Triple band sofa designed by Kem Weber and made by Lloyd. c. 1930s, streamlined form in re-chromed tubular steel, recent black leather cushions, 78" length x 43" depth x 33" height. *Photo courtesy Treadway Gallery.* $3,000-$4,000

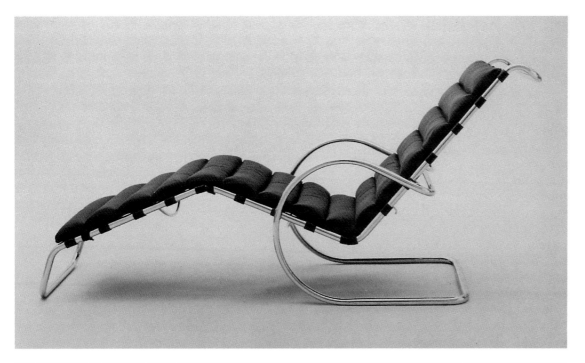

Lounge chair with arms designed by Mies van der Rohe 1927-1929, produced by Knoll Associates and part of the Knoll Studio Mies van der Rohe MR Collection, 70" length x 25 1/2" width x 31 3/4" height. *Photo courtesy Knoll.*

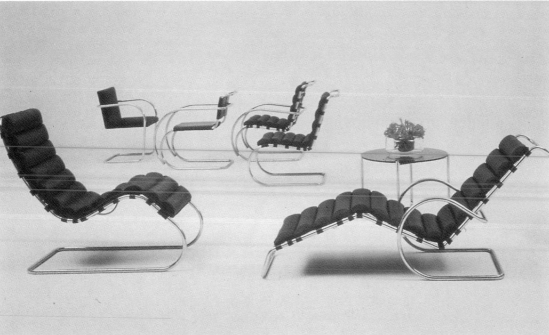

Knoll Studio Mies van der Rohe MR Collection: left, armless lounge chair; right, lounge chair with arms; center, arm chairs. *Photo courtesy Knoll.*

Catenary group: four Catenary seats and a glass top coffee table designed by George Nelson for Herman Miller, c. 1963. *Photo courtesy Herman Miller.*

Chaise lounge designed in 1968 by Charles and Ray Eames for Herman Miller, black aluminum frame, six urethane foam cushions and two loose cushions upholstered in black leather, 76 1/2" length x 17 1/2" width x 28" height. *Photo courtesy Treadway Gallery.* $1,500-$2,000

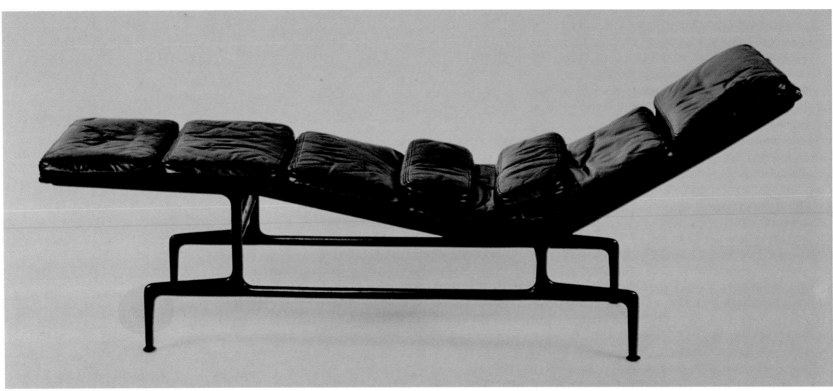

Sling sofa designed by George Nelson for Herman Miller in 1963, chromed tubular steel base and frame, black leather upholstery, urethane foam cushions reintroduced in the herman miller for the home, 32" depth x 87" length x 30" height. *Photo courtesy Herman Miller.* $2,000-$2,500

Chaise designed by George Nelson for Herman Miller, c. 1954. *Photo courtesy Herman Miller.*

Marshmallow sofa designed by Irving Harper for George Nelson Associates in 1956, produced by Herman Miller in limited quantities until 1965, of eighteen orange upholstered cushions fastened to bars, connected to a black tubular steel frame, a mid-century classic, 51" width x 30" depth x 33" height. *Photo courtesy Treadway Gallery.* $9,000-$12,000

Marshmallow sofa with alternating black and white naugahyde cushions. *Photo courtesy Treadway Gallery.* $9,000-$12,000

Opposite
"Listen to Me" chaise designed by Edward Wormley for Dunbar in 1947, of white maple and cherry construction, curved channel upholstered seat and back on laminated wood legs, joined by circular rods and x-form tension cable, metal label, 6' 3" length, identical example in collection of the Montreal Museum of Decorative Arts. *Photo © 1993 Sotheby's, Inc., courtesy Sotheby's New York.* $6,000-$9,000

Opposite

Rare wire sofa designed by Charles and Ray Eames in 1951, button-tufted three-section cushions supported by a wire frame, raised on strut-like supports and four shaped wooden feet, not produced commercially, and one of four examples known to have been made by Don Albinson. *Photo ©1993 Sotheby's, Inc., private collection, courtesy Massimo Martino S.A.-Lugano.* $30,000-$40,000

Lounge chair and ottoman designed by George Nelson for Herman Miller, the armless chair with clip-on table with white laminate top, reupholstered in black fabric, brushed steel legs; chair/table 45" width x 28" height; ottoman 26" width x 29" length x 15" height. *Photo courtesy Treadway Gallery.* $1,000-$1,500

Sofa designed by George Nelson for Herman Miller, plum upholstered seat and back cushions, white enameled metal frame, 72" width x 30" depth x 28" height. *Photo courtesy Treadway Gallery.* $600-$800

Chadwick Modular seating designed by Don Chadwick in 1974 and made by Herman Miller, in use at the Beachwood Branch of the Cuyahoga County Public Library. This design was selected by *Interior Design* as one of the 46 most influential modern furnishings of the past 50 years.

Front and side views of Chadwick Modular seating.

Swan chair designed by Arne Jacobsen and made by Fritz Hansen, on aluminum pedestal base, 29" width x 24" depth x 30" height. *Photo courtesy Treadway Gallery.* $600-$800

Swan settee designed by Arne Jacobsen in 1958 and made by Fritz Hansen, Denmark, biomorphic fiberglass shell reupholstered in deep blue wool, aluminum base, label, 56" width x 26" depth x 30" height. *Photo courtesy of Treadway Gallery.* $2,000-$2,500

Hans Wegner Papa Bear chair and ottoman, sculptural upholstered form on wooden legs, with inset wooden armrests, chair 36" width x 29" depth x 38" height; ottoman 27" width x 16" depth x 16" height. *Photo courtesy Treadway Gallery.* $1,000-$1,500

Vladimir Kagan armchair, upholstered in textured fabric, sculpted birch legs, 30" width x 34" depth x 28" height. *Photo courtesy Treadway Gallery.* $600-$800

Grasshopper chair, the first design by Eero Saarinen for Knoll Associates, in the late 1940s, bent birch arms and legs, reupholstered in dull green, 26 1/2" width x 32" depth x 34" height. *Photo courtesy Treadway Gallery.* $1,000-$1,500

Kangaroo chair designed by George Nelson for Herman Miller, c. 1956, olive green upholstery, brushed steel frame, 36" width x 24" depth x 39" height. *Photo courtesy Treadway Gallery.* $1,500-$2,000

Armchair designed by Alexander Girard for Herman Miller, c. 1969, cast aluminum frame, winged chair upholstered in beige and olive green with vivid blue seat cushion, 40" width x 30" depth x 26" height. *Photo courtesy Treadway Gallery.* $900-$1,200

Aluminum Group chair designed by Charles and Ray Eames for Herman Miller, high-back lounge chair with black channeled naugahyde upholstery, cloth headrest, tilt and swivel mechanism, 26" width x 24" depth x 36" height. *Photo courtesy Treadway Gallery.* $300-$500

No. 670 lounge chair and ottoman designed by Charles and Ray Eames for Herman Miller, introduced in 1956 of rosewood plywood, black leather down-filled cushions and armrests, mounted on five-pronged cast aluminum base; chair 32 3/4" width x 32 3/4" depth x 32 3/4" height; ottoman 26" width x 21" depth x 16" height. *Photo courtesy Treadway Gallery.* $2,000-$2,500

Pair of aluminum lounge chairs, c. 1960, attributed to Donald Deskey, blue and gold striped upholstery, swollen and tapering aluminum frame, disc feet, "Contemporary Interiors" label, 30 1/2" x 23 1/2" x 33". *Photo courtesy Skinner, Inc.* $400-$500 each

Armchair designed by Paul László for Herman Miller, c. 1949, low padded back with winged sides, deep cushioned seat joined by wide cushioned arms, four short legs, reupholstered in brown and beige striped fabric, 27" height. *Photo courtesy Christie's New York.* $700-$900

Pair of asymmetrical tub chairs upholstered in black velour with zebra stripe cushions and interior, a fabric pattern often used by Aino Aalto in the 1930s, 36" width x 36" depth x 25" height. $300-$500 each

Sculptural group designed by Pierre Paulin for Artifort, c. 1960s, orange upholstery over foam and metal frames, Ribbon chair on lacquered base, labels:
Tongue chairs, 36" width x 34" depth x 24" height. $700-$900 each.
Ribbon chair, 40" width x 20" depth x 27" height. $1,500-$2,000.
Ottoman, 20" diameter x 13" height. *Photo courtesy Treadway Gallery.* $200-$300

Pierre Paulin Ribbon chairs: left, rust upholstery on black lacquered base; right, magenta upholstery on white lacquered base. $1,500-$2,000 each

Cleopatra sofa designed by Geoffrey Harcourt for Artifort, sculptural molded foam upholstered in hot pink fabric, on metal casters, 74" width x 34" depth x 26" height. *Photo courtesy Treadway Gallery.* $2,000-$3,000

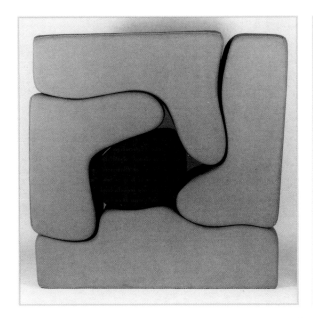

Three Frank Gehry Easy Edges laminated cardboard side chairs c. 1971, 15 1/4" width x 33 1/2" height. *Photo courtesy Skinner, Inc.* $1,000-$1,500 each

Malitte seating system designed by Surrealist painter Roberto Sebastian Matta in 1966, produced by Gavina, Italy (1966-1968) and by Knoll International (1968-1974), blocks of polyurethane foam, orange stretch wool upholstery, cobalt blue center piece, 64" width x 25" depth x 63" height total. *Photo courtesy Skinner, Inc.* $1,500-$2,500

Malitte seating group opened. *Photo courtesy Skinner, Inc.*

Herman Miller Modular seating group, c. 1973, benches,
chairs, couches, and tables. *Photo courtesy Herman Miller.*

Frank Lloyd Wright hinged church pew, designed for the Unitarian Church, Sherwood Hills, Wisconsin, c. 1947, shaped rectangular top hinged to a rectangular seat raised on low tapering legs, 42" length. *Photo ©1993 Sotheby's, Inc., courtesy Sotheby's New York.* $1,000-$1,500

Pair of lucite chairs by Erwine Laverne, produced by Laverne Originals, New York (1957-c. 1972), part of the Invisible Group, clear plastic chairs with high backs and scoop-shaped seats, on inverted circular bases, 37" height. *Photo courtesy Christie's New York.* $1,000-$1,500 each

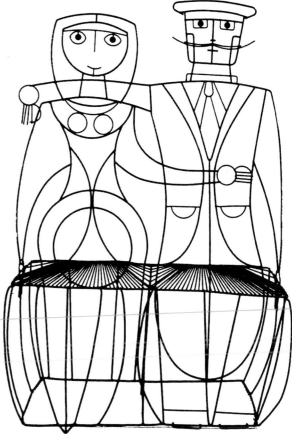

John Risley bench, whimsical figural wire construction of seated couple, 34" width x 16" depth x 51" height. *Photo courtesy Treadway Gallery.* $1,500-$2,000

Construction Case Study

Charles and Ray Eames 670-671 Lounge chair and ottoman made by Herman Miller. *Photo Earl Woods, courtesy Herman Miller.*

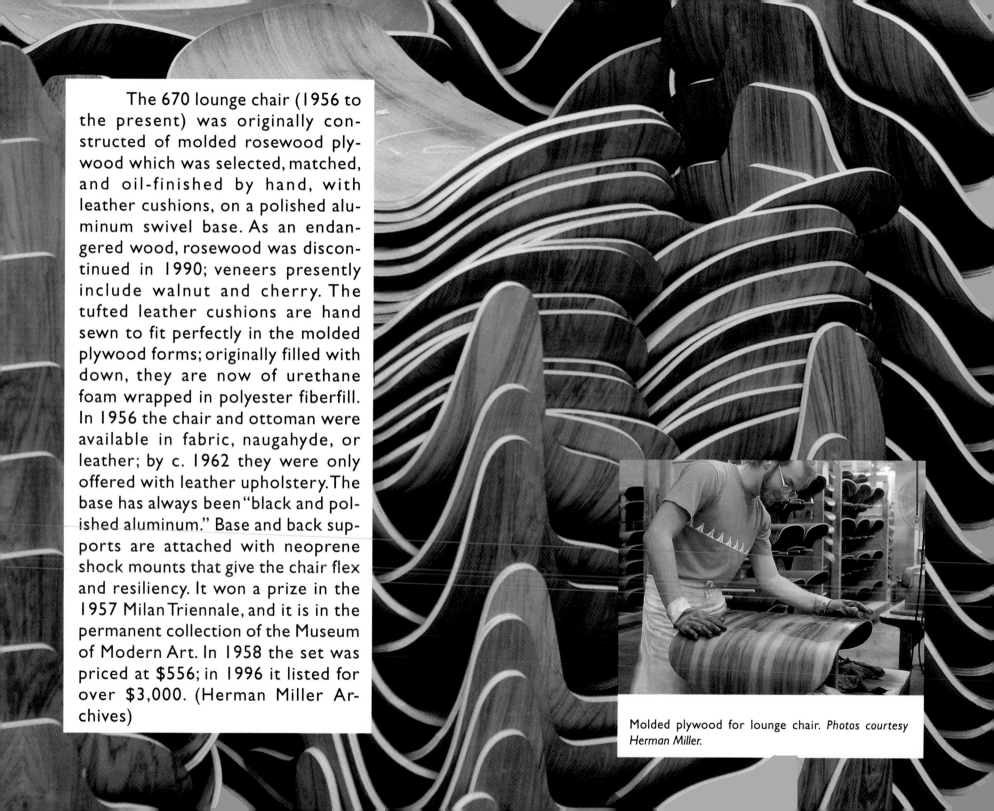

The 670 lounge chair (1956 to the present) was originally constructed of molded rosewood plywood which was selected, matched, and oil-finished by hand, with leather cushions, on a polished aluminum swivel base. As an endangered wood, rosewood was discontinued in 1990; veneers presently include walnut and cherry. The tufted leather cushions are hand sewn to fit perfectly in the molded plywood forms; originally filled with down, they are now of urethane foam wrapped in polyester fiberfill. In 1956 the chair and ottoman were available in fabric, naugahyde, or leather; by c. 1962 they were only offered with leather upholstery. The base has always been "black and polished aluminum." Base and back supports are attached with neoprene shock mounts that give the chair flex and resiliency. It won a prize in the 1957 Milan Triennale, and it is in the permanent collection of the Museum of Modern Art. In 1958 the set was priced at $556; in 1996 it listed for over $3,000. (Herman Miller Archives)

Molded plywood for lounge chair. *Photos courtesy Herman Miller.*

122

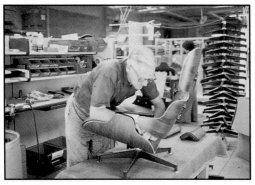
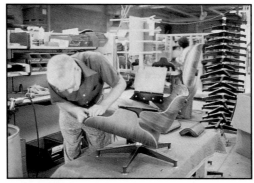

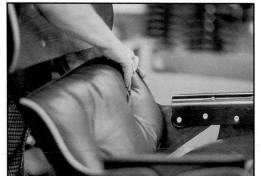

Tables

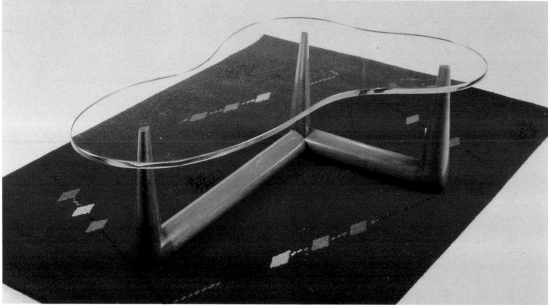

Isamu Noguchi coffee table, manufactured by Herman Miller from 1948 to 1973 and reintroduced in 1984, freeform triangular glass top with pale green edge, on birch wood base of two freeform supports, 50" length x 36" depth x 16" height; on '50s machine woven wool carpet with abstract pattern in red, gold, dull green, black, and off-white, label "Made in India," 49" width x 72" length. *Photo courtesy Treadway Gallery.* $1,500-$2,500; $300-$500

T. H. Robsjohn-Gibbings coffee table, manufactured by Widdicomb, circa late 1940s, walnut base of three up-side-down legs supporting a biomorphic shape glass top, 54" length x 33" depth x 17" height; on red carpet with black, blue, and tan diamond shapes, made in Brazil, 55" width x 78" length. *Photo courtesy Treadway Gallery.* $1,500-$2,500; $700-$900

Coffee table designed by Edward J. Wormley for Dunbar, freeform glass top supported on three walnut legs joined by triangular bronze stretcher, 16 1/2" height. *Photo courtesy Christie's New York.* $1,500-$2,000

Coffee table with freeform top of walnut veneer with freeform glass insert, on four asymmetrical x-stretcher legs, 57" length x 39" width x 16" height. $600-$800

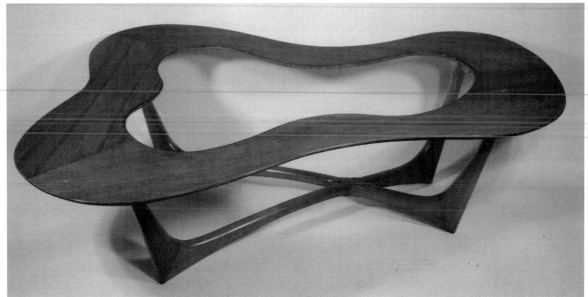

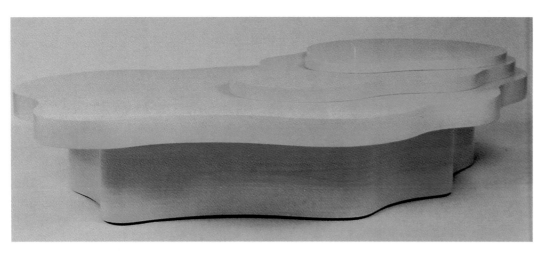

Biomorphic table after a design by Robsjohn-Gibbings, massive four-tiered wooden table with blond finish, 74" length x 53" depth x 16" height. *Photo courtesy Treadway Gallery.* $1,500-$2,000

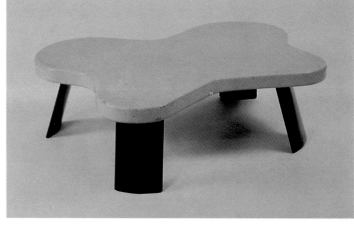

Paul Frankl coffee table manufactured by Johnson Furniture Co., c. 1949, biomorphic cream-colored cork top on splayed mahogany legs, also available with mahogany legs and lacquered pine top, 48" length x 36" depth x 14" height. *Photo courtesy Treadway Gallery.* $900-$1,200

Charles and Ray Eames ETR Surfboard table, produced from 1951 to 1964 by Herman Miller, black laminated top with laminated plywood beveled sides, black wire cage legs, 89" length x 29 1/2" depth x 10" height. *Photo courtesy Treadway Gallery.* $1,500-$2,500

Richard Schultz Petal table manufactured by Knoll (1960-1964), of segmented wooden top on eight-pronged enameled pedestal base, 42" diameter x 28" height. *Photo courtesy Treadway Gallery.* $900-$1,200

Warren Platner side table manufactured by Knoll, walnut top on circular wire base, 20" diameter x 18" height. *Photo courtesy Treadway Gallery.* $300-$500

Florence Knoll occasional table, manufactured by Knoll, circular gray marble top attached to steel disc, attached to four-legged pedestal base, 36" diameter x 17" height. *Photo courtesy Treadway Gallery.* $600-$800

Eero Saarinen dinette table manufactured by Knoll, polished marble top on white enameled metal pedestal base, label, 36" diameter x 27 1/2" height. *Photo courtesy Treadway Gallery.* $700-$900

Pair of George Nelson end tables, designed in 1954, off-white laminated tops on dark brown swag leg pedestal bases, 17" diameter x 22" height. *Photo courtesy Treadway Gallery.* $200-$300 each

George Nelson end table made by Herman Miller. *Photo courtesy Herman Miller.*

George Nelson end table with planter unit on top and storage drawer in front, with attached lamp, made by Herman Miller, c. 1951. *Photo courtesy Herman Miller.* $300-$400

Charles and Ray Eames Dish table, manufactured by Evans Products, distributed by Herman Miller, c. 1946, birch plywood top on tapered molded wooden legs, label, 34" diameter x 15" height. *Photo courtesy Treadway Gallery.* $700-$900

Mid-century style contemporary coffee table, arched aluminum legs and stretchers, red enameled feet, oval perforated aluminum top, 36" length x 22" width x 20" height. *Photo courtesy Treadway Gallery.* $300-$500

Charles and Ray Eames dinette table manufactured by Herman Miller, square white laminated plywood top on collapsible chromed metal legs, 34" square x 29" height. *Photo courtesy Treadway Gallery.* $600-$800

Hans Wegner dining table, oak drop leaf table with curved legs, brass swag locking mechanism, brand, closed 50" length x 34" width x 28" height, opens to 93 1/2". *Photo courtesy Treadway Gallery.* $1,000-$1,500

Left, three Gilbert Rohde nesting tables manufactured by Troy Sunshade Co., c. 1930, black lacquered wooden tops on square and tubular chromed metal frames, tallest 22" width x 11" depth x 22" height. $500-$700

Center, pair of Wolfgang Hoffman side tables manufactured by Howell, c. 1930s, two-tiered black lacquered wooden semicircular shelves on banded chromed metal frames, labels, 24" width x 12" depth x 22" height. $500-$700

Right, Art Deco tochére, c. 1930s, all chrome construction with flared shades, 12" diameter x 63" height. *Photo courtesy Treadway Gallery.* $300-$400

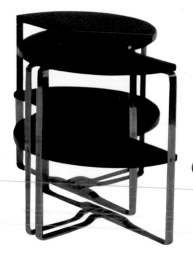

Pair of Jens Risom side tables, white laminate tops on black wrought iron circular bases, 14" diameter x 21" height *Photo courtesy Treadway Gallery.* $300-$500

Heywood Wakefield drop leaf dining table, c. 1950s, solid birch top on three arched birch legs, two leaves, closed 40" width x 28" depth x 29" height. *Photo courtesy Treadway Gallery.* $700-$900

Primavera wood gateleg table designed by George Nelson for Herman Miller, c. 1949, rectangular top with wide aprons with notched joins, on six straight legs joined by side stretchers, marked "model 4656," closed 18 1/2" x 39" width x 30" height. *Photo courtesy Christie's New York.* $1,500-$2,000

Robsjohn-Gibbings nest of tables manufactured by Widdicomb, blond finished mahogany and veneered, decal, 26" length x 23" width x 24" height. *Photo courtesy Skinner, Inc.* $700-$900

Tables 135

Storage

Art Deco bedroom set, c. 1930s, streamline aluminum construction with purplish-blue vinyl top and front, tall chest 34" width x 19" depth x 40" height; low chest 43" width x 19" depth x 34" height; twin headboards 39" width; with Art Deco table lamp with spun aluminum base and shade, 13" width x 15" height. *Photo courtesy Treadway Gallery.* $1,000-$1,500 set; $100-$200 lamp

Gilbert Rohde dresser made by Herman Miller, c. 1933, five-drawer chest in blond wood accented with dark parallel lines on top and sides, deep orange catalin ball pulls, tubular chromed base, metal tag and paper label, 33" width x 18 1/2" depth x 46" height. *Photo courtesy Treadway Gallery.* $2,000-$2,500

Gilbert Rohde bed made by Herman Miller, in blond wood accented with dark parallel lines, chromed legs, 39" width x 82" length x 32" height. *Photo courtesy Treadway Gallery.* $400-$600

Gilbert Rohde secretary made by Herman Miller, c. 1940, four curved doors at the bottom and drop-front desk with compartments at top, 66" width x 15" depth x 72" height. $1,500-$2,000

Walter Dorwin Teague table clock, manufactured by General Electric, c. 1930s, stepped chromed base with lighted clock face with Art Deco numerals, 8" width x 4" depth x 8" height. $200-$300

Henry Dreyfuss thermos and tray made by American Thermos Co., c. 1930s, enameled metal with brushed aluminum. $300-$500

Rockwell Kent ice bucket by Chase, 9" x 9". *Photo courtesy Treadway Gallery.* $300-$500

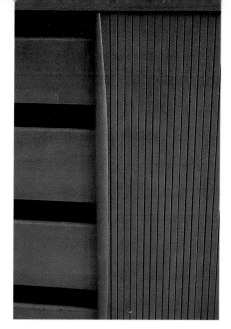

Detail of tambour door.

Heywood Wakefield buffet of solid birch, four drawers and two doors, 48" width x 18" depth x 34" height; matching two-piece china cabinet with one drawer and two doors on base, three shelves with sliding glass doors on top, 34" width x 18" depth x 67" height. *Photo courtesy Treadway Gallery.* $600-$800; $600-$800

Heywood-Wakefield chest with four drawers and tambour doors, 35" width x 19" depth x 31 1/2" height. *Courtesy Studio Moderne.* $600-$800

Heywood Wakefield bedroom set, c. 1950, champagne finish five-drawer bureau, mirrored vanity with stool, and bedside stand, branded and stamped marks, bureau 34" width x 19 1/2" depth x 46" height. *Photo courtesy Skinner, Inc.* $1,200-$1,800

Mid-century Danish Modern walnut bureau by Illums Bolighus, Copenhagen, four long drawers, metal tag, 39 1/2" width x 18" depth x 34" height; with matching walnut vanity, drop-front top fitted with retractable mirror and small compartments and drawers, two wide drawers on bottom, metal tag and stamped, 39 1/2" width x 18" depth x 34" height. *Photo courtesy Skinner, Inc.* $500-$700; $500-$700

These small teak cabinets with white pulls were designed to go with rosewood group cases. They could be placed on top of cabinets, either with or without three-inch tapered legs. These cabinets are also shown on the white pedestal base found with Nelson pedestal tables.

George Nelson jewelry chest made by Herman Miller, with six drawers, teak sides and rosewood drawer fronts, white laminate top, four-prong pedestal base, 30" width x 13" depth x 26 1/2" height. $2,000-$2,500

George Nelson miniature chest, produced by Herman Miller from 1954 to 1963, flat case with six drawers with white fronts, originally of rosewood and reissued in teak for herman miller for the home, 1994. *Photo courtesy Herman Miller.*

George Nelson miniature chest, produced by Herman Miller from 1954 to 1963, rosewood with white laminate top, six drawers with white enamelled metal pulls, metal tag, stamped 224, 30" width x 14" depth x 5 3/4" height. *Photo courtesy Christie's New York.* $1,000-$1,500

George Nelson Thin Edge cabinet manufactured by Herman Miller, rosewood cabinet with four drawers and two doors, porcelain pulls, aluminum legs, 56" width x 18" depth x 30" height. *Photo courtesy Treadway Gallery.* $2,000-$3,000

George Nelson Thin Edge cabinet manufactured by Herman Miller, teak with aluminum legs, drop-front with compartments and five small drawers, label, 56" width x 18" depth x 41" height. *Photo courtesy Treadway Gallery.* $2,000-$3,000

George Nelson Thin Edge vanity manufactured by Herman Miller, two four-drawer teak veneered cabinets with fold-down mirror, florescent light, and cosmetic compartments, label, 78" width x 18 1/2" depth x 27" height; with vanity stool made by Herman Miller, upholstered seat and black wooden legs, 22" width x 16" depth x 17" height. *Photo courtesy Treadway Gallery.* $1,000-$2,000; $150-$200

George Nelson cabinet manufactured by Herman Miller, walnut veneered case with five drawers and one door, silver-plated pulls, black ebonized legs, label, 40" width x 18 1/2" depth x 40" height. *Photo courtesy Treadway Gallery.* $800-$1,000

George Nelson cube, made by Herman Miller, one-drawer cabinet in blond wood with black wooden legs, chromed pull, 18" width x 18" depth x 24" height. *Photo courtesy Treadway Gallery.* $300-$400

George Nelson cabinet, made by Herman Miller in walnut veneer with wooden pulls, four drawers and one door, 34" width x 18 1/2" depth x 24" height. $500-$700

Greta von Nessen Anywhere lamp manufactured by Nessen Studios, c. 1952, blue enameled shade, cantilevered chromed base, 12" width x 9" depth x 14" height. *Photo courtesy Treadway Gallery.* $500-$700

Charles Eames ESU cabinet manufactured by Herman Miller, another variation with primary colored masonite panels, chromed angle iron, five wooden drawers, white fiberglass sliding doors, blond and black shelves. *Photo courtesy Treadway Gallery.* $9,000-$11,000

Charles and Ray Eames ESU 400 Series cabinet manufactured by Herman Miller, c. 1952, black angled iron frame with masonite panels of red, yellow, blue, black, and white, three wooden drawers, black sliding doors, 47" width x 16 1/2" depth x 58" height. *Photo courtesy Treadway Gallery.* $8,000-$10,000

George Nelson Primavera sideboard made by Herman Miller, c. 1949, four drawers and one door, four short legs, round wood knobs, model #4712, 56" length x 18 1/2" depth x 29 1/2" height. *Photo courtesy Christie's New York.* $1,000-$1,200

George Nelson rosewood dresser made by Herman Miller, cube form with four drawers, four chromed columnar feet, porcelain pulls, metal tag, 24 1/2" length x 27 3/4" height. *Photo courtesy Christie's New York.* $800-$1,000

Frank Lloyd Wright mahogany server made by Heritage Henredon Furniture, eight drawers and two doors, branded mark, 66" length x 20" depth x 66" width. *Photo courtesy Skinner, Inc.* $1,500-$2,000

Bookcase/cabinet designed by Paul McCobb for the Irwin collection, made by Calvin Furniture, upper case divided by four bronze supports with open bay, drawers, and compartments, the lower part with three accordion doors and five drawers, on six bronze legs and stretchers, metal tag, 71" width x 83" height. *Photo courtesy Christie's New York.* $1,200-$1,800

Paul McCobb sideboard, from Irwin collection made by Calvin Furniture, dark mahogany, two three-section folding doors covering shelves and two drawers, on brass legs and stretchers, marble top, metal tag, 60" width x 19" depth x 34" height. $1,000-$1,500

Jens Risom chests/dressers placed side by side: left, 54" width x 21" depth x 31 1/2" height; right 36" width, with metal label in drawer, assortment of mid-century glass and ceramic items on top. *Courtesy Studio Moderne.* $400-$600 each

Three-tiered cabinet, suspended sections with sliding glass doors, on wooden legs and supports, 41" width x 16" depth x 68" height. *Photo courtesy Treadway Gallery.* $600-$800

Office

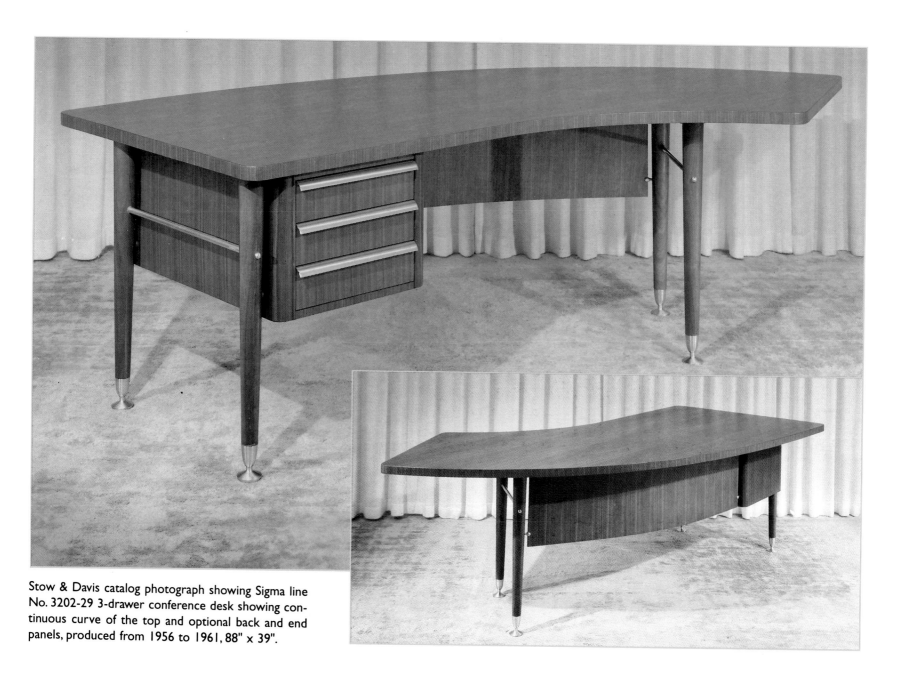

Stow & Davis catalog photograph showing Sigma line No. 3202-29 3-drawer conference desk showing continuous curve of the top and optional back and end panels, produced from 1956 to 1961, 88" x 39".

STOW DAVIS

(part of Steelcase since 1985)

The following black and white photographs were used in Stow Davis product brochures and catalogs in the 1950s and 1960s and are provided as a courtesy from Stow Davis.

Stow & Davis Sigma line No. 3202-30 desk with top in the form of a bent angle, also produced from 1956 to 1961, 86" x 40".

Stow & Davis Sigma line No. 3202-39 showing more frontal view and without optional back and end panels. *Photo by Grand Rapids Commercial Photo Co., courtesy Stow Davis.*

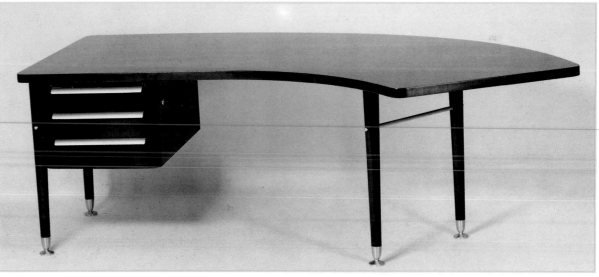

Stow & Davis Sigma items in American walnut with No. 6 Gunstock finish and brushed brass or brushed chrome hardware, produced from 1956 to 1961: 3202-29 desk; 3289-29 ceiling mounted light panel; 32A-32AS chairs with leather upholstery; 3247-72 wall mounted tambour cabinets; and 3227 cabinet with 72" top.

Sigma 3201-17 conference desk;
3247 120" tambour cabinet, and 32A
chairs, 1956-61.

Sigma 3201-17 desk with freeform top, suspended pedestals, file, and three box drawers, in American walnut, produced from 1956 to 1961, 100" x 42".

Sigma series No. 3202-40 desk with freeform top, produced from 1956 to 1961, 76" x 38".

Sigma series No. 3202-45 desk with rectangular top, produced from 1956 to 1961, 76" x 38".

Sigma series No. 3202-45 desk in blond finish with optional end panels, (1956-1961), 76" x 38".

Stow & Davis No. 6100 Custom Executive desk, with brushed chrome finish tubular steel frame, produced from 1959 to 1967. *Photo by Rook's Photo, courtesy of Stow & Davis.*

Stow & Davis Executive Predictor series No. 5601-36 executive desk with mirror chrome finish square post legs, produced from 1963 to 1964, 76" x 36".

Executive Predictor series No. 5604-36 desk with three-pronged attachment for round legs, produced from 1963 to 1964.

Executive Predictor in walnut with round legs and feet, with 56A armchair with leather inserts on arms, 1963-1964.

Stow & Davis Predictor II No. 5796-4 executive desk with side unit, squared tops rather than chamfered, and brushed chrome rather than mirror, produced from 1961-1967.

No. 5700 Predictor II desk with 64-A armchairs.

Executive Predictor office with 56-A chairs, 58-AS posture chair, 5601-47 desk, c. 1963-1964.

Executive Predictor office with upholstered chairs.

Stow & Davis Custom Executive office with No. 6040
credenza, produced 1959-1967.

Custom Executive series 6000/6100, 6041 credenza, produced from 1959 to 1967, 76 1/2" x 20" x 25 3/4" height.

Custom Executive No. 6002 desk with 7 drawers including file, back panel, 84" x 40".

Custom Executive No. 6098-36 desk with back panel (84" x 40") and side unit with 3 compartments, 1959-1967, total size 84" x 78".

Custom Executive No. 6008-25 table, 1959-1967.

Custom Executive No. 6011-13 conference table with shaped top and 2 pedestals, 120" x 48" along with 59A armchairs.

Stow & Davis No. 605A sofa, No. 6053 end table, No. 6008-25 executive table, No. 604S credenza, and No. 59AS executive swivel chair.

No. 6011-84 round conference table, 60" diameter x 29" height.

Stow & Davis office with No. 6100 desk with wood frame instead of metal.

No. 6102-47 desk, 76" x 36", designed to combine with 6100 credenza as a side unit and 68AS swivel chair, 1959-1967.

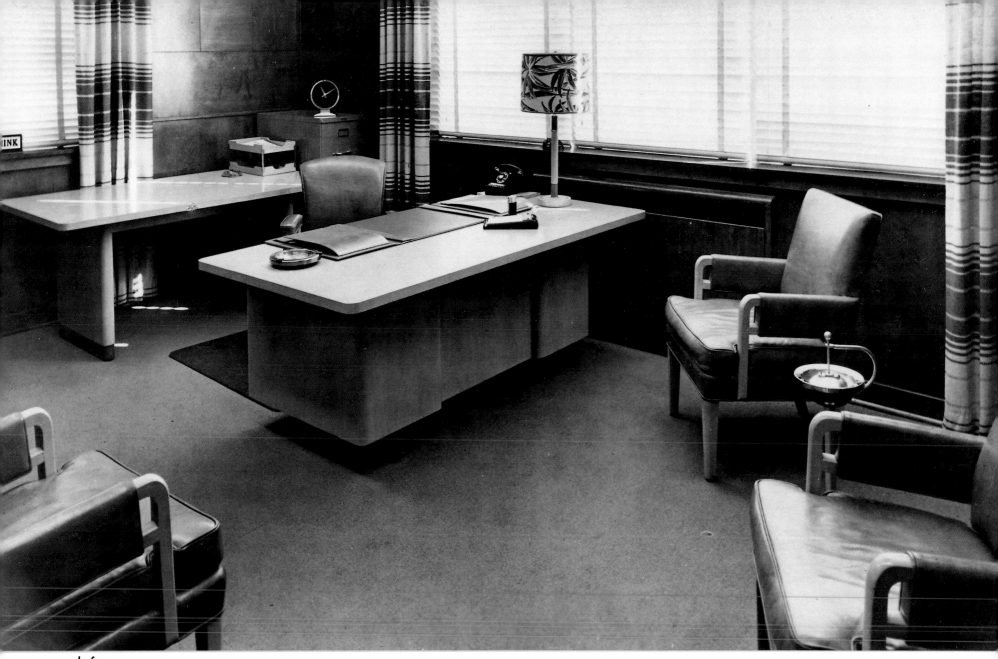

Left
Progression II: side table, No. 237A chair (front), No. 237AS desk chair, No. 21TCX cabinet (beside desk chair), and No. 2076 CDX desk, produced from 1952 to 1960.

Stow & Davis Harwood group office at the Olsen Transfer Co. in Green Bay, Wisconsin, featuring No. 2160 desk, 60" x 30" x 29".

Stow & Davis office with No. 2145H 96" credenza top on No. 21TCO cabinet, No. 66AS chair (behind desk), No. 236A chairs (front), and No. 2166D desk, 66" x 36" x 29".

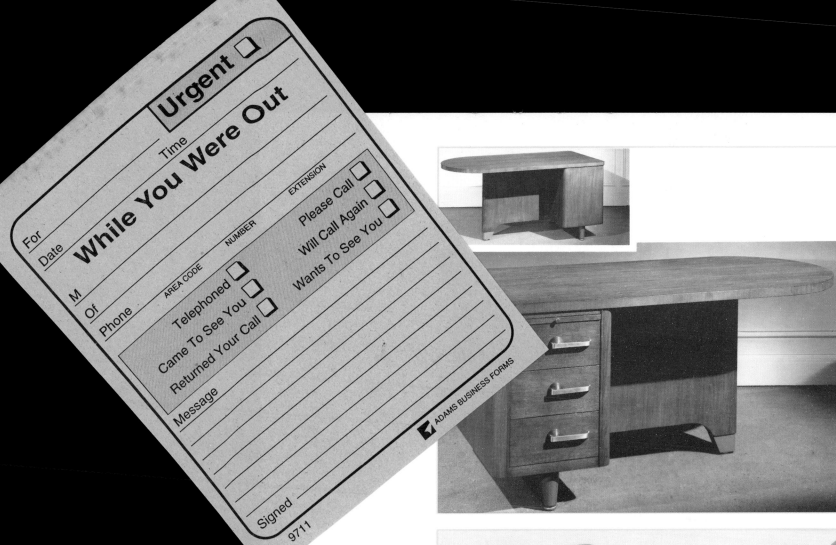

Front and back views of No. 2160CDX interviewing desk, 60" x 30" x 28 1/2" height.

Left, No. 22A chair; right, No. 22AS chair.

Front view of No. 2290FB freeform double pedestal desk with back panel, 90" x 49" x 29".

Opposite
Front and back views of Executive Group freeform desk No. 2269CD with light walnut top on dark walnut four-drawer pedestal and curved pedestal base, 69" x 42" x 29", 1952-1960.

No. 22 1/2 T table with curved double pedestal base, 60" x 26" x 15" height.

Table with freeform double pedestals, available in two sizes: No. 22-96PT, 96" x 42" x 29" or No. 22-120PT, 120" x 48" x 29".

Executive Group office with No. 60AS armchair and
No. 229OF desk in American walnut with light finish,
90" x 49" x 29", 1952-1960.

Stow & Davis office showing back view of freeform
double pedestal desk.

Painted metal and walnut desk and upholstered chair designed by Frank Lloyd Wright and manufactured by Metal Office Furniture Co. (Steelcase) for the S. C. Johnson Wax Administration Building in Racine, Wisconsin in 1938, a forerunner of systems furniture. *Photo courtesy Steelcase.*

Paladio desk designed by Gilbert Rohde and made by Herman Miller, c. 1940, with kidney-shaped top on double pedestal base wrapped in leatherette, with conical brass pulls, 54" width x 27" depth x 29" height. $1,500-$2,000

Side chair by industrial designer noted for his work in aluminum, Warren McArthur, c. 1930, of aluminum with red anodized accents, black vinyl seat, 16" square x 33" height. McArthur had a factory in Los Angeles, followed by Rome, New York, and then Bantam, Connecticut. $1,000-$1,500

Art Deco desk lamp designed by Kem Weber, made of patinated metal with glass finial, 9" diameter x 13" height. $400-$600

Zephyr clock designed by Kem Weber and made by Lawson, of streamlined form in patinated copper and chrome, with ball feet, 8" width x 3" depth x 4" height, c. 1930s. *Photo courtesy Treadway Gallery.* $300-$400

No. 4023 desk designed by Gilbert Rohde for Herman Miller, six-drawer kneehole desk in ash with brown lacquered wooden pulls, 49" width x 24" depth x 29" height. *Photo courtesy Treadway Gallery.* $1,000-$1,500

Desk designed by Eliel Saarinen for the Johnson Furniture Co., c. 1940s, bi-level birch with three drawers, curved wooden leg and metal hardware, 48" width x 20" depth x 31" height. $1,500-$2,000

Art Deco desk lamp of streamlined form in patinated copper with decorative brass knob, 11" diameter x 12" height. *Photo courtesy Treadway Gallery.* $300-$500

Heywood-Wakefield double pedestal M-315-W knee-hole desk with deep file drawer on left, designed by Count Alexis de Sakhnoffsky, prominent automobile stylist, in 1931, produced of solid birch from 1947 to 1949, 30" width x 24" depth x 30" height. $2,000-$2,500

Detail of desk drawer and streamlined pull.

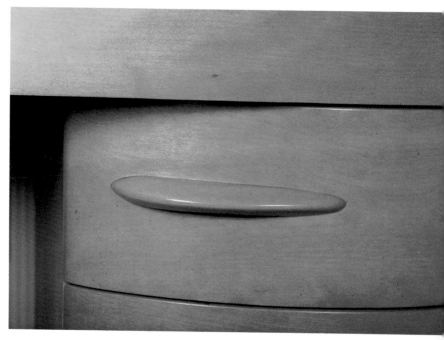

Heywood-Wakefield maple roll top desk in streamlined form on slender tapered square legs, top opens to reveal six compartments, 32" width x 24" depth x 33" height. *Photo courtesy Treadway Gallery.* $1,000-$1,500

Thin-Edge writing table designed by George Nelson for Herman Miller, c. 1954, veneered top with three drawers, white porcelain pulls, white double pedestal base, 42" width x 24" depth x 29" height. *Photo courtesy Treadway Gallery.* $8,000-$10,000

ESU desk designed by Charles and Ray Eames for Herman Miller, c. 1952, walnut plywood top on black angled iron frame, white masonite panels, three drawers, 60" width x 28" depth x 29" height. $2,000-$2,500

Two Dowel Leg chairs designed by Charles and Ray Eames for Herman Miller, an early wooden version of the Eiffel Tower base: behind desk with seafoam green Zenith shell, 24" width x 22" depth x 27" height; front with parchment swiveling Zenith shell, 25" width x 18" depth x 30" height, early labels. $500-$700 each

Italian desk lamp with pivoting brass arm and adjustable blue shade, on marble base, 6" diameter x 18" height. *Photo courtesy Treadway Gallery.* $200-$400

Left, Steelframe desk designed by George Nelson for Herman Miller, black angle iron frame with three drawers with blue fronts and gray sides, white laminate top, chrome pulls, 44" width x 17" depth x 29" height. $400-$600

Adjustable florescent '50s desk lamp, 8" width x 4" depth x 12" height. $100-$200

Center, Steelframe desk designed by George Nelson for Herman Miller, black angle iron frame with three drawers, white laminate top, chrome pulls, label, 42" width x 17" depth x 29" height. $400-$600

Right, pair of Steelframe end tables designed by George Nelson for Herman Miller with black enameled angle iron frame, white laminate tops and orange laminate shelves, 17" square x 22" height. *Photo courtesy Treadway Gallery.* $400-$600 pair

ESU desk designed by Charles and Ray Eames for Herman Miller, c. 1952, hollow plywood rectangular top on early angle iron legs, 60" width x 24" depth x 29" height. $2,000-$2,500

Eiffel Tower chair designed by Charles and Ray Eames for Herman Miller, black wire with black leather upholstery, on blond wood legs, label, 19" width x 17" depth x 31" height. $500-$700

Table clock with fused glass face by Frances and Michael Higgins on General Electric clock. $300-$400

Italian '50s desk lamp with adjustable brass arm, counterweights, pivoting blue metal shade, 8" diameter x 20" height. *Photo courtesy Treadway Gallery.* $300-$500

Executive Office Group (EOG) designed by Gilbert Rohde in 1942, marked the entry of Herman Miller into the office furniture market. *Photo courtesy Herman Miller.*

Black lacquered and iron desk designed by George Nelson for Herman Miller, c. 1955, flat top over three stacked drawers with concave round wood pulls on brass posts, raised on iron cylindrical frame, with manufacturer's labels, 29 1/2" height x 40" length x 23 3/4" width. *Photo courtesy Skinner, Inc.* $500-$1,000

Secretary desk designed by George Nelson for Herman Miller, four drawers in black finish, on tubular brushed chrome frame, 34" width x 16" depth x 24" height. *Photo courtesy Treadway Gallery.* $400-$600

Swag-legged desk and chair designed by George Nelson, by the far wall in an office with an EOG desk in the foreground, at the reception area of the Administration Building at Herman Miller Furniture Co., c. 1958. *Photo courtesy Herman Miller.*

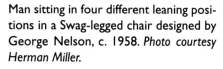

Man sitting in four different leaning positions in a Swag-legged chair designed by George Nelson, c. 1958. *Photo courtesy Herman Miller.*

Nelson desk. *Photo courtesy Herman Miller.*

Blond mahogany kneehole desk designed by George Nelson for Herman Miller, rectangular top supported by two side pedestals with drawers, on four cylindrical chrome legs, with curved chrome handles, 29 3/4" height x 60" length. *Photo courtesy Christie's New York.* $1,000-$1,500

Opposite

Wire and steel desk chair designed by Charles Eames for Herman Miller, c. 1953, with scoop back grid of white plastic-covered wire, on black legs, and chromed steel pedestal flaring to four legs ending in wheels, 32" height. *Photo courtesy Christie's New York.* $800-$1,000

Wood-grained conference table with two support prongs to each H leg designed by George Nelson for Herman Miller, c. 1969. *Photo courtesy Herman Miller.*

Herman Miller Action Office, introduced 1964: stand-up desk with foot rest and perching stool (right); can be combined with other Action Office components such as communications carrel (center), sit-down desk, mobile conference table, and storage unit. *Photo Louis Reens, courtesy Herman Miller.*

Right

Herman Miller roll top desk with foot rail, blue sides, chrome legs, and wood tambour top, part of Action Office 1, 1964. *Photo courtesy Herman Miller.* $800-$1,200

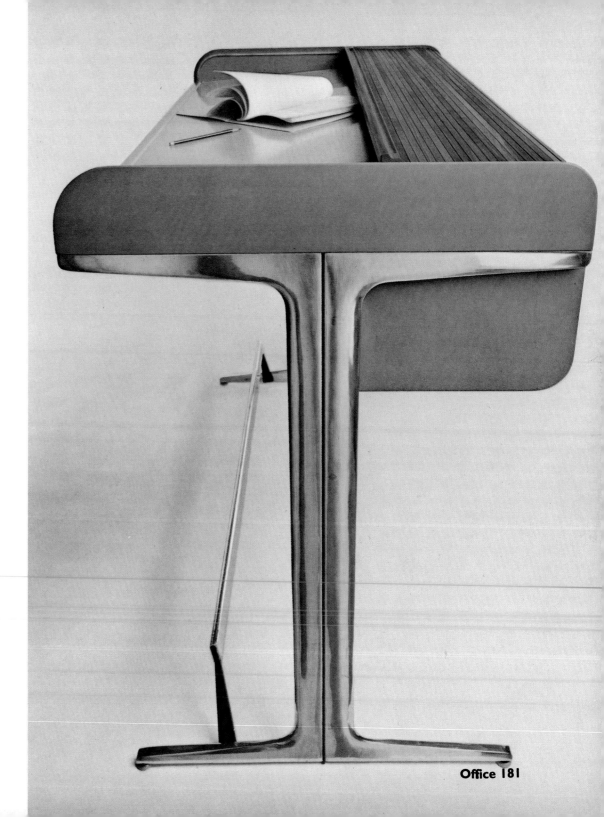

The Little Toy, designed by Charles and Ray Eames for Tigrett Enterprises, c. 1952, a variation of The Toy, comprised of a box of modular square and triangular panels of heavy brightly colored cardboard with pierced corners, square and triangular wire frames, and small pieces of colored, coated bell wire. $1,000-$1,500

Group of House of Cards sets designed by Charles and Ray Eames: one set of Computer House of Cards designed for IBM for the World's Fair in Osaka, Japan in 1970; one partial set of House of Cards produced from 1952 to 1962; one pictorial set of House of Cards; one pictorial set of 2nd House of Cards; and a partial set of Giant House of Cards, c. 1962. *Photo ©1993 Sotheby's, Inc., private collection, courtesy Massimo Martino S.A.-Lugano.* $500-$700

Left, Block clock designed by George Nelson Associates for Howard Miller Clock Co., yellow-orange lacquered wood block hour markers, yellow metal center, black hands, 12" diameter. $400-$600

Right, Asterisk clock designed by George Nelson Associates for Howard Miller, black metal with white metal hands, 10 1/2" diameter. $300-$500

Asterisk clock designed by George Nelson Associates
for Howard Miller, black metal body with black hands,
10" diameter. $300-$500

Asterisk clock designed by George Nelson Associates
for Howard Miller, yellow metal body with black hands,
10 1/2" diameter. $300-$500

Clock designed by George Nelson Associates for
Howard Miller, wood spokes radiating from central
brass disc, white push pin markers and white hands,
14" diameter. $600-$800

Ball clock, model #4755 designed by George Nelson Associates for Howard Miller, birch "atom" balls on brass spokes, brass central disc, black hands. $300-$500

Left, model #2239 brass and wood spool wall clock designed by George Nelson Associates for Howard Miller, twelve waisted wooden spokes radiating from brass face, white triangular and orange hand, 23" diameter. $300-$500

Right, version of #4755 Ball clock with white face, 13" diameter. *Photo courtesy Christie's New York.* $300-$500

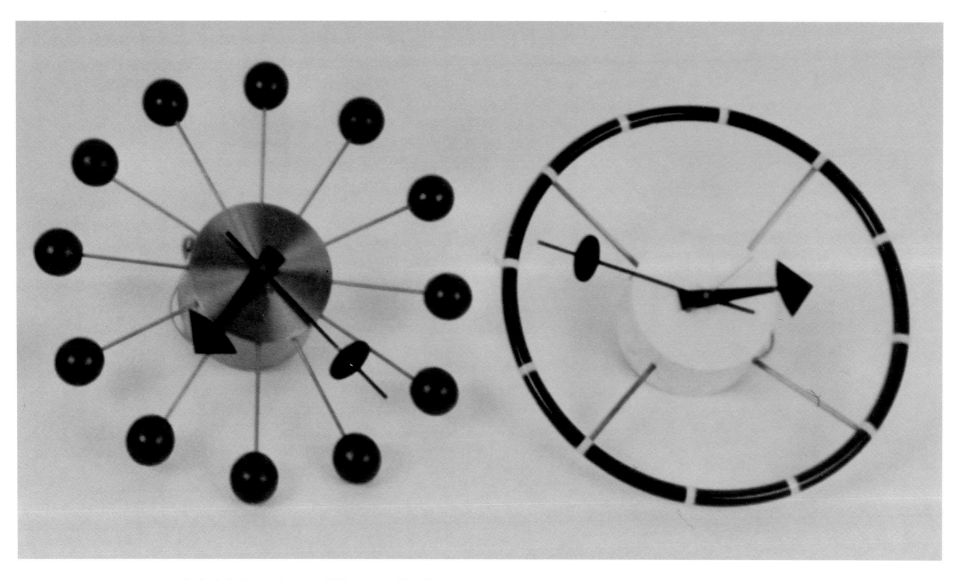

Left, Ball clock, Model #4755 designed by George Nelson Associates for Howard Miller, black wood "atom" balls on brass spokes, black hands, 13" diameter. $300-$500

Right, Steering Wheel clock designed by George Nelson Associates for Howard Miller, white center, black metal outer ring with white tape hour markers, black hands, 12" diameter. $300-$500

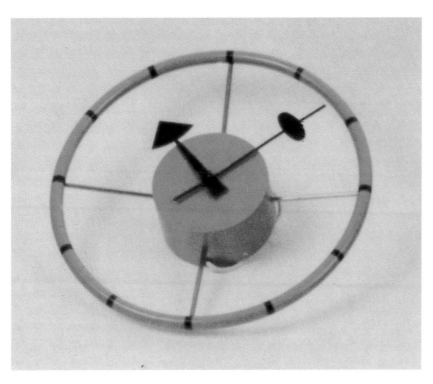

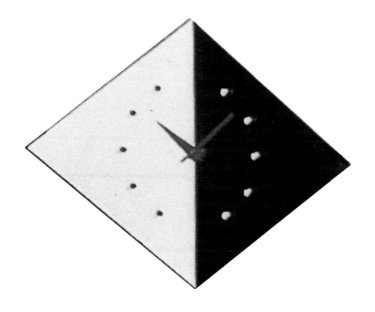

Steering Wheel clock designed by George Nelson Associates for Howard Miller, orange enameled metal center and outer ring, black tape hour markers, black hands, label, 12" diameter. $300-$500

Kite clock designed by George Nelson Associates for Howard Miller, diamond-shaped sheet metal painted black and white, red hands, wooden peg hour markers, 21" x 17" height. *Photos courtesy Treadway Gallery.* $600-$800

Wall clock designed by Georges Briard and made by Glass Guild, of glass mosaic in blues and greens. $100-$150

Model #4765 chronopack walnut and brass desk clock on brass ring foot, designed by George Nelson Associates for Howard Miller. *Photo courtesy Christie's New York.* $400-$600

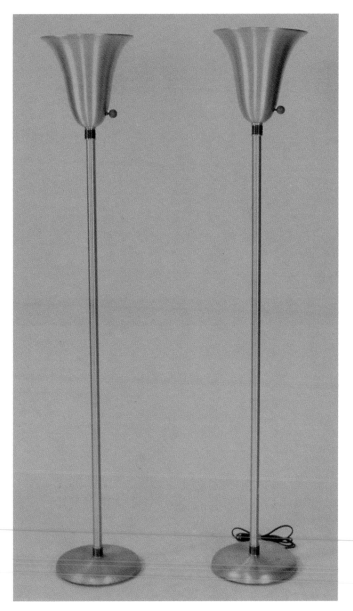

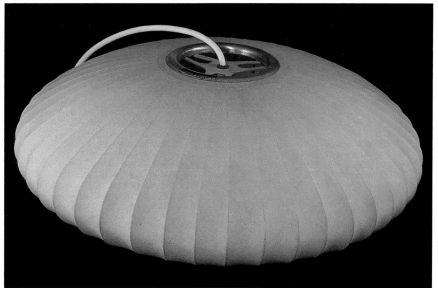

Bubble lamp designed by George Nelson Associates for the Howard Miller Clock Co., label. $150-$250

Pair of floor lamps by Kurt Versen, each of gray enameled metal shade on gooseneck frame. *Photo courtesy Treadway Gallery.* $300-$400

Pair of torchére floor lamps designed by RusselWright, c. 1940s, spun aluminum with wrapped trim on top and bottom of poles, wooden ball switch, 11" diameter x 65" height. *Photo courtesy Treadway Gallery.* $700-$900

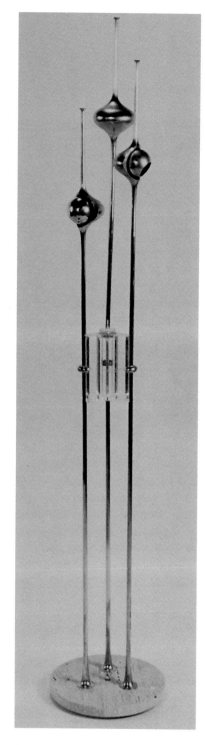

Artluce floor lamp, c. 1960s, three attenuated brass rods with ovoid hollows with pivoting brass sockets, circular marble base, 74" height. *Photo courtesy Treadway Gallery.* $2,000-$2,500

Artluce floor lamp, three adjustable shades in white, gray, and black with single chrome pole on tripod base, leather grips on lamp arms, stamped "Made in Italy," 33" width x 59" height. *Photo courtesy Treadway Gallery.* $1,500-$2,000

Floor lamp attributed to Russel Wright, c. 1940s, c-shaped on domed base with adjustable white parchment shade, 36" diameter x 56" height. $400-$600. Eero Saarinen Grasshopper chair, left. *Photo courtesy Treadway Gallery.*

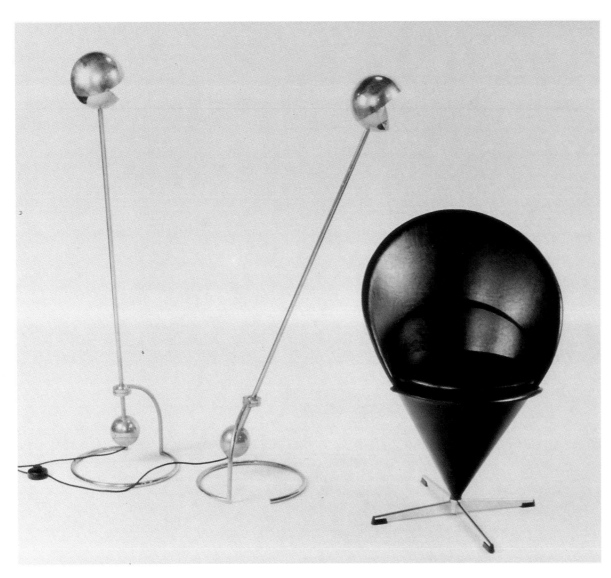

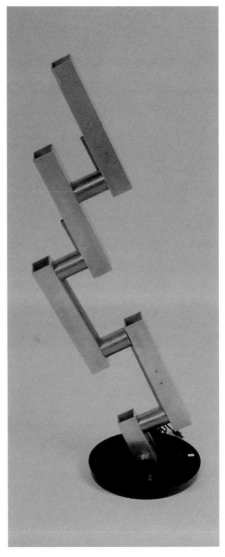

Pair of Austrian floor lamps, each with chrome-plated globular adjustable shade on single pole with circular base, paper label "made in Austria," 14" diameter x 53" height. Verner Panton Cone chair, right. *Photo courtesy Treadway Gallery.* $500-$700; $800-$1,200

'60s floor lamp, sculptural design of aluminum and brass on a black wooden base, 12" diameter x 43" height. *Photo courtesy Treadway Gallery.* $300-$500

Pierre Garuche hanging lamp, black enameled metal shade with white perforated reflector on a brass arm, 45" length x 28" height. *Photo courtesy Treadway Gallery.* $700-$900

Table lamp attributed to Frank Gehry, corrugated cardboard with chrome band at top and bottom, 17" diameter x 30" height; on occasional table designed by T. H. Robsjohn-Gibbings for Widdicomb, with wooden circular top on three intersecting legs, 30" diameter x 25" height. *Photo courtesy Treadway Gallery.* $300-$400; $300-$500

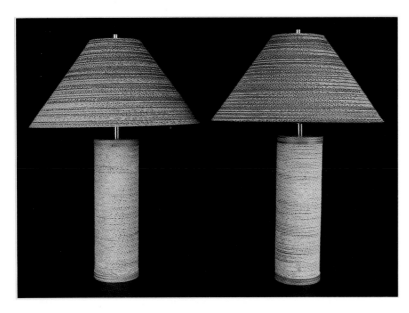

Pair of Frank Gehry "Easy Edges" table lamps, c. 1972, each with stack laminated cardboard shade and base, with plywood ends, 20" diameter x 26 1/2" height. *Photo courtesy Skinner, Inc.* $1,000-$1,500

'60s table lamp, yellow enameled metal shade and conical pedestal base, lights on top and under shade, 20" diameter x 19" height; on La Fonda coffee table by Charles Eames for Herman Miller, patterned top designed by Alexander Girard with outer rubber ring, four-pronged aluminum base, 30" diameter x 17" height. *Photo courtesy Treadway Gallery.* $200-$300; $200-$300

Lightolier table lamp with rectangular base of dark brown bisque porcelain, with gold Facade pattern designed and signed by Georges Briard, made by Hyalyn for Lightolier, c.1960. *Photo courtesy Georges Briard.* $150-$250

Eames molded plywood folding screen, reintroduced herman miller for the home. *Photo Phil Schaafsma, courtesy Herman Miller.*

Richter Originals wall plaques, each with hollow plastic relief of yellow, orange, and red Fifties glass bottles, in brown wood frame, 18 1/2" x 32 1/2" with paper label "Richter Artcraft, Toledo, Ohio 1963." $50-$75 each

Harris Strong ceramic tile plaques

Single tile panel showing rooftops and chimney pots and two women with parasols, in blues, green, yellow, and red-orange with chunky dark lines; on oiled walnut plaque, 121 in ink on back, 10 1/2" square. $175-$275

Single tile panel of person pulling a cart downhill in city scene, in turquoise, lavender, green, red, and chunky dark lines; on oiled walnut plaque, 122 in ink on back, 10 1/2" square. $175-$275

Single tile panel of three people walking on a path with bridge in background in blues, red, chunky dark lines; on oiled walnut plaque, 123 in ink on back, 10 1/2" square. $175-$275

Example of Harris Strong paper label.

Single tile of four frogs in browns, teal, and yellow, outlined in black; mounted on navy linen with matching frame, Group E #32, 10 3/4" square. $60-$100

Single tile with two fish in browns with white eyes on black background; mounted on linen in oak frame, 10 3/4" square. $60-$100

Single tile of stylized penguins in blue, green, yellow, rust, and black on white ground; mounted on linen in black frame, Group E #78, 10 3/4" square. $60-$100

Single tile night scene of buildings in earthtones outlined in white, against a black starry sky; mounted on linen in oak frame, Group A #42, 10 3/4" square. $70-$100

Single tile of church buildings in earth tones outlined in white, against a black starry sky; mounted on linen in oak frame, Group A #44, 10 3/4" square. $70-$100

Single tile of trees with black trunks and autumn leaves on white ground; mounted on linen with oak frame, signed STRONG, 10 3/4" square. $60-$100

Example of Harris Strong signature.

Single tile of lakeside houses and boats a night in yellow, olive, blue, and black; mounted on linen with oak frame, signed STRONG, 10 3/4" square. $60-$100

Single tile close-up view of church dome and buildings in blue, yellow, and brown; mounted in walnut frame, Group L #73, 9 3/4" square. $60-$100

Single tile of close-up of multi-colored village scene with three figures on a cobblestone street; in walnut frame, Group L #74, 9 3/4" square. $60-$100

Irregularly-shaped tiles of queen or princess wearing multi-colored Klimt-like robe; on oiled walnut plaque, 41 1/4" x 9 1/2", signed HARRIS G. STRONG on back. $400-$500

Irregularly-shaped tiles depicting a jester or falconer with multi-colored geometric costume; on oiled walnut, 41 1/4" x 9 1/2" signed HARRIS G. STRONG on back. $400-$500

Two-tile vertical panel with abstract design in shades of vivid orange and black chunky lines; mounted on 29" oiled walnut plaque, tile 18" x 6". $50-$75

Opposite
Two-tile vertical panel with abstract design, in vivid oranges and black, mounted on 29" oiled walnut plaque, tile 18" x 6". $50-$75

Six-tile vertical panel of sailboats in a bay and mountains on the horizon in blues, greens, and yellow; framed in chestnut with gold trim, 21 1/2" x 15 1/2", label on back # 141. $300-$400

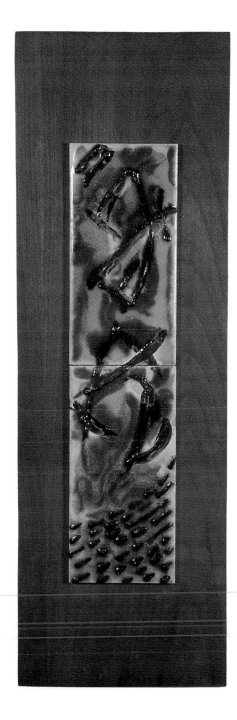

Opposite
Three-tile horizontal panel of multi-colored buildings and smoke stacks; walnut frame with gold trim, 10" x 22", #313, signed STRONG on front. $200-$300

Five-tile horizontal panel picturing a parade of Medieval figures in blues, greens, and purples; mounted on oiled walnut plaque, 12" x 36", ink mark 540 on back. $300-$400

Fifteen-tile vertical panel depicting Machu Picchu and alpacas in turquoise and blues; linen mat and wood frame, 35 3/4" x 23 3/4". $600-$700

Example of heart-shaped wire hangers.

Four-tile horizontal panel of park scene with two women with parasols in horse-drawn carriage in autumn leaf colors; on oiled walnut plaque, 24" x 11". $250-$350

Four-tile horizontal panel of cubist skyline in vivid oranges, yellow, and brown; on oiled walnut plaque, 36" x 9". $200-$300

Opposite
Three-tile horizontal panel of country scene with birds in flight and fish in a river in turquoise blues; black wood frame, 22" x 10", paper label, #320 on back. $250-$350

Three-tile horizontal panel of country scene with man herding cows in blues and greens; black wood frame, 22" x 10", paper label, #321 on back. $250-$350

Groupings

Warren Platner wire seating group, designed 1966, shown in the City Spire Condominium, New York City, in Knoll Studio Platner Collection. *Photo courtesy Knoll.*

Left, rare Charles and Ray Eames molded plywood child's table, c. 1945, inspired by Marcel Breuer's molded plywood table of 1936, the molded rectangular plywood top continuing to tapered legs, 26 1/2" length x 15 1/2" width x 16 1/2" height. *Photo ©1993 Sotheby's, Inc., private collection, courtesy Massimo Martino S. A.-Lugano.* $2,500-$4,000

Right, rare Charles and Ray Eames molded plywood child's chair, c. 1945, the T-shaped back with pierced heart shape joined to a molded seat with four tapering legs. ©1993 Sotheby's, Inc. $3,000-$4,000

George Nelson Black Frame Group made by Herman Miller: round dining table and four chairs set for dinner, and a marble topped double buffet, c. 1961. *Photo courtesy Herman Miller.*

Set of four Eames DCW chairs made by Herman Miller, of laminated and molded walnut plywood, 19" width x 21" depth x 29" height. $1,000-$1,500

Nelson Swag-leg dinette table made by Herman Miller, c. 1956, rectangular walnut top on chrome swag leg base, 54" length x 32" width x 29" height. *Photo courtesy Treadway Gallery.* $1,000-$1,500

Opposite

George Nelson cabinet made by Herman Miller, c. 1950, four drawers and one door of ebonized wood, on brushed steel hairpin legs, 56" width x 18" depth x 29" height. $1,000-$1,500

Charles and Ray Eames DCM chairs made by Herman Miller, molded red aniline dyed plywood seats and backs, on tubular chromed frames; with similar DCM chair with ebonized seat and back, 19" width x 21" depth x 29" height. $400-$500 each; $200-$300

Charles and Ray Eames folding dinette table made by Herman Miller, richly grained plywood top on black metal folding legs, 34" square x 29" height. *Photo courtesy Treadway Gallery.* $800-$1,000

George Nakashima coffee table made by Widdicomb, walnut slat construction on three tapered legs, 84" length x 29" depth x 13" height. $900-$1,200

Charles and Ray Eames LCM chair, molded rosewood plywood seat and back on chrome frame, rare variation, 22" width x 20" depth x 27" height. *Photo courtesy Treadway Gallery.* $800-$1,000

Lloyd dinette set, c. 1930s, black laminate top on chromed metal base, with four tubular metal chairs with red-orange upholstery and lacquered wooden armrests; table 36" square x 29" height; chairs 21" width x 17" depth x 31" height. *Photo courtesy Treadway Gallery.* $500-$700 set

Set of four Eames DCM chairs made by Herman Miller, seats and backs in original red aniline dye, legs and spine of chromed solid steel, early labels, 19" width x 19" depth x 29" height. $2,500-$3,000

Eames folding table made by Herman Miller, white laminate top with laminated plywood sides, chromed solid steel legs that fold in, and black naugahyde handle under top, 34" square x 29" height. $600-$800

Eames Hang It All, c. 1953, white enameled iron and painted wood balls, 20" width x 15" height. *Photo courtesy Treadway Gallery.* $800-$1,000

Robsjohn-Gibbings dining table and chairs, manufactured by Widdicomb, c. 1940, two armchairs (one pictured) and four side chairs (three pictured) in original pumpkin upholstery, with rectangular walnut table with curved legs; chairs 22" width x 18" depth x 34" height; table 62" length x 39" width x 29" height. *Photo courtesy Treadway Gallery.* $2,000-$3,000 set

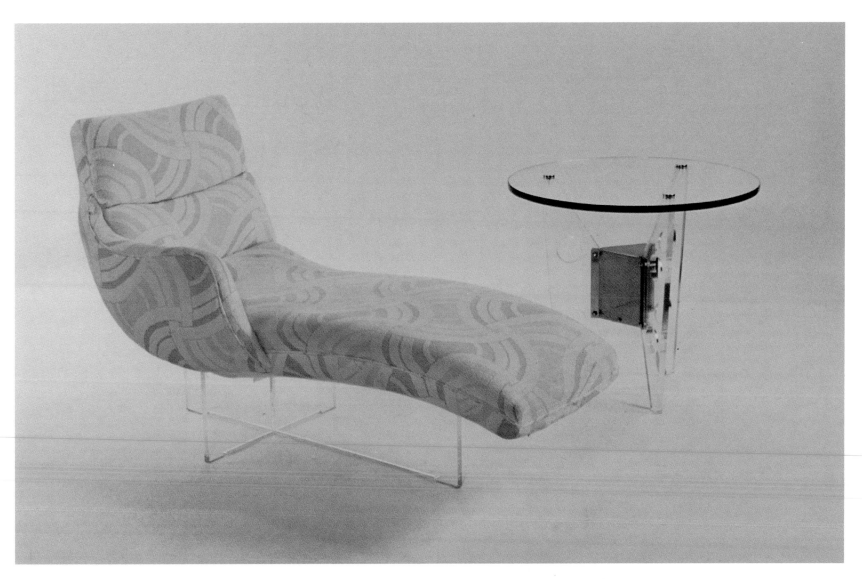

Vladimir Kagan chaise lounge, c. 1960s, biomorphic form in original off-white patterned upholstery, on lucite base, label KAGEN MULTIPLES BY PREVIEW, 64" length x 26" width x 33" height. $1,500-$2,000

Modern occasional table, c. 1960s, three lighted triangular lucite legs with pierced holes, glass top, 29" diameter x 25" height. *Photo courtesy Treadway Gallery.* $500-$700

Alexander Girard occasional table, manufactured by Herman Miller, c. 1969, patterned marble top on cast aluminum base, 20" square. $700-$900

Gae Aulenti La Ruspa lamp, c. 1960s, white metal double shade on pivoting arm, 12" width x 13" depth x 22" height. $1,000-$1,500

Alexander Girard chair, manufactured by Herman Miller, c. 1969, original green and black upholstery, cast aluminum frame, 27" width x 30" depth x 26" height. *Photo courtesy Treadway Gallery.* $500-$700

'50s chair with curved seat and back, of laminated wooden strips, 30" width x 22" depth x 29" height. $200-$300

Edward Fields carpet in vibrant orange, red, and white geometric design, all wool, 95" x 60". $700-$900

'60s lamp with adjustable chromed pole, black ball lamp, and reflector, 32" width x 70" height. *Photo courtesy Treadway Gallery.* $300-$400

Eero Saarinen Grasshopper chair, by Knoll, 30" width x 32" depth x 34" height. $1,000-$1,500

Isamu Noguchi coffee table, by Herman Miller, 50" width x 36" depth x 15" height. $2,000-$3,000

'50s carpet, made in Brazil, 80" x 56". $700-$900

George Nelson chest, made by Herman Miller, five drawers with silver-plated pulls, hairpin legs, 40" width x 18" depth x 39" height. $800-$1,000

'50s floor lamp with adjustable arm and pivoting red shade, mounted on rough-edged marble base, 15" diameter x 60" height. $500-$700

Ben Seibel desk lamp, distributed by Raymor, c. 1951, black metal ring supporting pivoting frame with red perforated shade, 7" diameter x 26" height. *Photo courtesy Treadway Gallery.* $300-$500

George Nelson tray table, made by Herman Miller, adjustable base, wood veneer top with curled edges, 15" square x 20" height. $400-$600

George Nelson daybed, made by Herman Miller, backless version with birch frame and foam cushions in red, orange, and brown upholstery, matching bolster cushions, 75" length x 33" width x 26" height. $1,000-$1,500

Paul McCobb Planner group chest on bench, manufactured by Winchedon, c. 1950s, six-drawer birch cabinet with stainless ring pulls, on birch bench, 48" width x 18" depth x 39" height. $400-$600

Pierre Jeanneret folding lounge chair, with red and black wool cushions, 24" width x 30" depth x 18" height. *Photo courtesy Treadway Gallery.* $300-$400

Left, Gio Ponti walnut dresser made by Singer, c. 1950s, eight drawers with large rectangular wooden handles. $1,500-$2,000

O-Luce desk lamp, black enameled metal with brass accents, 7" diameter x 23" height, extends to 60" as shown on example at right. $300-$500

Right, Gio Ponti walnut dresser made by Singer, c. 1950s, four drawers with large rectangular handles. $1,000-$1,500

Center, Verner Panton Cone chair of bent steel wire cage construction, upholstered seat, 23" width x 24" depth x 32" height. *Photo courtesy Treadway Gallery.* $1,000-$1,500

George Nelson daybed made by Herman Miller, wood frame with primavera finish, hairpin metal legs, reupholstered in red fabric, 75" width x 34" depth x 27" height. $1,500-$2,000

'50s carpet, made in Brazil of flat woven wool with geometric design on dark green ground, 91" x 63". $800-$1,000

George Nelson slat bench, made by Herman Miller, ebonized wooden top and legs, 72" length x 18" depth x 14" height. $700-$900

Lightolier floor lamp, gray enameled tripod frame with adjustable cone shades in orange, white, and gray, 22" diameter x 60" height. $300-$500

Charles and Ray Eames rocker made by Herman Miller, black wire struts on birch rockers, bright red fiberglass shell, 24" width x 27" depth x 27" height. $600-$800

Richard Schultz Petal table, made by Knoll, c. 1960, white lacquered segmented wooden top on delicate base, 16" diameter x 19" height. *Photo courtesy Treadway Gallery.* $400-$500

Arteluce floor lamp, three-armed adjustable lamp with shades in primary colors, on brass frame, early tripod base, 46" width x 62" height. $1,800-$2,200

George Nelson Thin Edge cabinet made by Herman Miller, rosewood with six drawers, porcelain pulls, aluminum legs, original condition, 47" width x 18" depth x 31" height. $2,000-$3,000

George Nelson table clock made by Howard Miller, c. 1958, round white and green enameled metal body with lucite bubble cover over accordion folded face, battery operated, 6" diameter x 9" height. $400-$600

Isamu Noguchi table lamp made by Knoll, c. 1950s, cherry wood frame, floating fiberglass shade, 7" diameter x 16" height. $800-$1,000

George Nelson Coconut chair made by Herman Miller, triangular white metal shell, chromed legs, in original purple upholstery, 40" width x 34" depth x 33" height. *Photo courtesy Treadway Gallery.* $1,500-$2,000

Charles and Ray Eames folding screen made by Herman Miller 1946-1955, custom 3/4 height screen, eight molded red aniline dyed plywood sections on flexible canvas hinges, rare example, 78" width x 46" height. $3,000-$5,000

Eames ESU cabinet made by Herman Miller, c. 1952, black angle iron frame, colored masonite side panels, black perforated metal back, three wooden drawers, 24" width x 16" depth x 32" height. $2,500-$3,500

Eames DCM chair made by Herman Miller, molded rosewood plywood seat and back on black metal frame, 19" width x 20" depth x 29" height. *Photo courtesy Treadway Gallery.* $200-$300

Eames folding screen made by Herman Miller 1946-
1955, six molded birch plywood sections on flexible
canvas hinges, 61" width x 68" height. $2,500-$3,500

French Kite lamp c. 1950s, brass tripod floor lamp with
black enamel shade and ached perforated metal reflector, 16" width x 15" depth x 60" height. $2,000-$2,500

Eames ESU cabinet made by Herman Miller, c. 1954,
two-tiered storage unit with angle iron frame, birch
top and drawers, colored masonite panels, white fiberglass sliding doors, original condition, 47" width x 16"
depth x 32" height. *Photo courtesy Treadway Gallery.*
$2,000-$2,500

Pair of Charles and Ray Eames laminated ash four-paneled folding screens, c. 1946, each of four u-form molded sections with canvas hinges, 68" height x 40" width. Generally available as six-panel screens, this custom-ordered pair is unusual because of the size and matched veneers. $4,000-$6,000

Pair of Charles and Ray Eames molded laminated plywood LCW chairs, c. 1946. $1,800-$2,500

Molded plywood and chrome-plated metal coffee table by Charles and Ray Eames for Herman Miller, c. 1946, dished circular top raised on four angled cylindrical legs, 33 1/4" diameter x 16 1/4" height. *Photo ©1993 Sotheby's, Inc., courtesy Sotheby's New York.* $1,200-$1,800

Eero Saarinen Womb chair and ottoman, designed in 1946 and made by Knoll, upholstered molded fiberglass shell in organic shape, on black metal legs, reupholstered in Knoll black and white fabric; chair 39" width x 34" depth x 35" height; ottoman 25" width x 22" depth x 15" height. $1,200-$1,800

Paul Frankl coffee table made by Johnson Furniture, c. 1940s, biomorphic cork top on splayed dark wooden legs, 36" width x 47" length x 15" height. $2,000-$2,500

Arne Jacobsen Egg chair made by Fritz Hansen, c. 1960s, upholstered molded fiberglass shell on aluminum swivel base, original light green fabric, 40" width x 30" depth x 35" height. $2,000-$2,500

Pair of Alvar Aalto stacking stools made by Artek, c. 1950, circular birch top on three molded birch legs, 15" diameter x 17" height. *Photo courtesy Treadway Gallery.* $300-$350 each

Eames rocker, Frankl table, and Verner Panton wire
Cone chair, c. 1959, on four-pronged metal base. *Photo
courtesy Treadway Gallery.* $800-$1,200

Pair of Eames Eiffel Tower chairs made by Herman Miller, of molded fiberglass, upholstered in black and white checkered fabric by Alexander Girard, on Eiffel Tower bases, 25" width x 25" depth x 30" height. $300-$400 each

'50s French wrought iron coat rack, with wooden balls of primary colors, string wrap tripod base, 20" diameter x 64" height. $500-$700

'50s French wall rack, S-curved wrought iron bar with wooden balls in primary colors, 29" width x 4" depth x 5" height. $300-$500

Isamu Noguchi dinette table made by Knoll, white laminate top on chromed criss-cross wire struts, coated black iron ring base, 36" diameter x 29" height. *Photo courtesy Treadway Gallery.* $3,000-$3,500

George Nelson Steel Frame lounge chair made by Herman Miller, c. 1953, channeled black wool upholstery on flat steel frame, 27" width x 27" depth x 41" height. $2,000-$2,500

Edward Wormley Janus table made by Dunbar, c. 1956, Tiffany glass tile top on walnut pedestal tripod base with brass tips, rare example, 10" square x 23" height. *Photo courtesy Treadway Gallery.* $1,000-$1,500

Eames lounge chair and ottoman made by Herman Miller, black leather cushions in molded rosewood shells, mounted on cast aluminum five-pronged base; chair 34" width x 28" depth x 33" height; ottoman 26" width x 24" depth x 16" height. $1,000-$1,500

Nelson slat bench made by Herman Miller, primavera finish with ebonized legs, 56" length x 18" depth x 14" height. $1,000-$1,500

Frances and Michael Higgins fused glass plaques, 7" x 14". $300-$500 each

'50s French wall rack of zigzag shape in black wrought iron with wooden balls in primary colors, resembling Charles and Ray Eames "Hang-It-All" by Herman Miller. $200-$300

Nelson Bubble floor lamp made by Howard Miller, elongated bubble on wire frame, mounted on metal tripod base, 12" diameter x 36" height. $300-$400

Eames Dish table, made by Evans Products and distributed by Herman Miller, c. 1946, birch plywood top on tapered molded wooden legs, 34" diameter x 15" height. *Photo courtesy Treadway Gallery.* $700-$900

Three Eames molded plywood lounges and ottomans
in the living room at Marigold Lodge. *Photo Nick Merrick,
courtesy Herman Miller.*

Library stair attributed to Edward Dodd, c. 1972, of laminated bent bird's eye maple and maple, 22" width x 66" height. $300-$500

Danish Modern bookcase by Illums Bolighus, Copenhagen, medium finish, five adjustable shelves, metal tag, 35 1/2" width x 10 5/8" depth x 33" height. $400-$600

Danish Modern coffee table by Illums Bolighus, medium finish, metal tag, 60" length x 20" width x 15 1/4" height. *Photo courtesy Skinner, Inc.* $300-$500

Heywood Wakefield upholstered armchair, design attributed to Count Alexis De Sakhnoffsky, c. 1935, 22 1/4" width x 35" height. $200-$300

Heywood Wakefield buffet, #M593, c. 1954, shaped top over long drawer and three short drawer, two cabinet doors, decal and stencils, 54" width x 18" depth x 34" height. *Photo courtesy Skinner, Inc.* $600-$800

Resources

The following are some United States sources — auction houses, manufacturers, and distributers — that supply circa fifties furniture or related items. Many additional sources, especially retail stores, advertise in the magazine Echoes Report, Box 2321, Mashpee, MA 02649, (508) 428-2324.

Manufacturers

Cassina USA Inc.
155 East 56th St.
New York, NY 10022
(516) 423-4560
(800) 770-3568

Herman Miller, Inc.
855 East Main Ave. Box 302
Zeeland, MI 49464-0302
(800) 646-4400
herman miller for the home

Front entrance to Suite Lorain Antiques, one of many sources for a range of mid-century items from designer to kitsch. *Courtesy Suite Lorain*

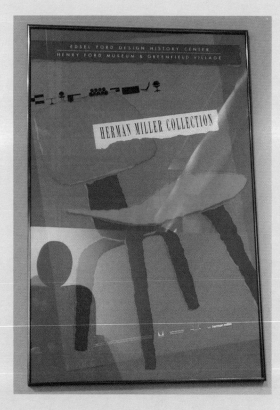

Poster for Herman Miller Collection, on display at Herman Miller Pavilion in Grandville, Michigan.

Herman Miller Pavilion furniture showroom.

Two Eames sofas and a Noguchi table at the Rotunda of the Grandville Pavilion. *Photo Nick Merrick, courtesy Herman Miller*

Toledo table and chairs from the Knoll Studio Pensi Collection, 1986-1988, lightweight anodized aluminum chairs (stack 8 high), round and square tables in 8 sizes, with 3 stainless steel top finishes, on display at the Knoll facility in Grand Rapids.

Heywood-Wakefield
180 NE 39th St., Suite 104
Miami, FL 33137
(305) 576-4240

Knoll
105 Wooster St.
New York, NY 10012
(800) 445-5045
fax (212) 207-2202
Knoll Studio

Lightolier
631 Airport Rd.
Fall River, MA 02720
(508) 679-8131

Thonet Madison
403 Meacham Rd.
Statesville, NC 28677
(800) 551-6702
Marcel Breuer

Auction Houses

Christie's
502 Park Ave.
New York, NY 10022
(212) 546-1000
catalogs (718) 784-1480

David Rago
17 S. Main St.
Lambertville, NJ 08530
(609) 397-9374
Chris Kennedy
(800) 366-3376

Skinner, Inc.
63 Park Plaza
Boston, MA 02116
(617) 350-5400
357 Main St.
Bolton, MA 01740
(508) 779-6241

Sotheby's, Inc.
1334 York Ave.
New York, NY 10021
(212) 606-7000
catalogs (800) 444-3709

Treadway Gallery, Inc.
2029 Madison Rd.
Cincinnati, OH 45208
(513) 321-6742
fax (513) 871-7722
modern auctions held in Chicago

Select Bibliography

Abercrombie, Stanley. *George Nelson: the Design of Modern Design*. Cambridge: MIT Press, 1995.

Blitzer, William. former president of Lightolier, telephone interview, Jan. 1996; typescript.

Byars, Mel. *The Design Encyclopedia*. New York: John Wiley & Sons, 1994.

Caplan, Ralph. *The Designs of Herman Miller*. New York: Whitney Library of Design, 1976.

Christie's New York. auction catalog *American Design 1920-1960*. Sept. 26 & 27, 1986.

Collins, Philip. *Pastime: Telling Time from 1879 to 1969*. San Francisco: Chronicle, 1993.

Conway, Hazel. *Ernest Race*. London: Design Council, 1982.

Cyran, Carol A. "Alvar Aalto Furniture: The Fundamental Years." *Echoes Report* 3 (Spring 1995).

_____. "Edward Wormley." *Echoes Report* 4 (Summer 1995).

_____. "Gilbert Rohde: Innovator, Entrepreneur, Catalyst." *Echoes Report* 4 (Winter 1995).

DePree, Hugh. *Business as Usual*. Zeeland, Michigan: Herman Miller, 1986.

Detroit Institute of Arts. *Design in America: The Cranbrook Vision 1925-1950*. New York: Harry N. Abrams, 1983.

Dormer, Peter. *Design Since 1945*. London: Thames and Hudson, 1993.

Droste, Magdalena, et al. *Marcel Breuer Design*. Köln, Germany: Taschen, 1992.

Edwards, Clive D. *Twentieth-century Furniture: Materials, Manufacture and Markets*. Manchester and New York: Manchester University Press, 1994.

Eidelberg, Martin, ed. *Design 1935-1965: What Modern Was*. New York: Harry N. Abrams, 1991.

Emery, Marc. *Furniture by Architects*. New York: Harry N. Abrams, 1983; expanded edition 1988.

Fehrman, Cherie and Kenneth Fehrman. *Postwar Interior Design 1945-1960*. New York: Van Nostrand Reinhold, 1987.

Fiell, Charlotte & Peter. *Modern Chairs*. Köln, Germany: Taschen, 1993.

_____. *Modern Furniture Classics Since 1945*. Washington, D.C.: A.I.A. Press, 1991.

Gandy, Charles D. and Susan Zimmermann-Stedham. *Comtemporary Classics: Furniture of the Masters*. New York: Whitney Library of Design, 1990 (originally McGraw-Hill, 1981).

Garner, Philippe. *Twentieth-Century Furniture*. New York: Van Nostrand Reinhold, 1980.

Glaeser, Ludwig. *Ludwig Mies van der Rohe: Furniture and Furniture Drawings*. New York: Musuem of Modern Art, 1977.

Greenberg, Cara. *Mid-Century Modern: Furniture of the 1950s*. New York: Harmony, 1984; reprinted 1995.

Heinz, Thomas A. *Frank Lloyd Wright Furniture Portfolio*. Layton, Utah: Gibbs Smith, 1993.

Hiesinger, Kathryn B. & George H. Marcus. *Landmarks of Twentieth-Century Design: An Illustrated Handbook*. New York: Abbeville, 1993.

Hennessey, William J. *Russel Wright: American Designer*. New York: MIT Press, 1983.

Herman Miller. Corporate archives.

"Herman Miller for the Home." *Interior Design* 64 (Dec. 1993).

Herman Miller Furniture Co. *The Herman Miller Collection*. catalog. Zeeland, Michigan: Herman Miller Furniture Co., 1952; reprinted New York: Acanthus Press, 1995.

_____. *Herman Miller for the Home*. catalog. Zeeland, Michigan: Herman Miller, 1995.

Horn, Richard. *Fifties Style*. New York: Friedman/Fairfax, 1993.

Jackson, Lesley. *The New Look: Design in the Fifties*. New York: Thames Hudson, 1991.

_____. *Contemporary Architecture and Interiors of the 1950s*. London: Phaidon, 1994.

Jespersen, Mark. "Interview with Jens Risom." *Echoes Report* 4 (Fall 1995).

Julier, Guy. *Encyclopedia of 20th Century Design and Designers*. New York: Thames and Hudson, 1993.

Kaskovich, Steve. "Changing Times: Howard Miller's Clock Co's prosperity spans generations." *Detroit News* (Oct. 30, 1989): 1D & 4D.

Kirkham, Pat. *Charles and Ray Eames: Designers of the Twentieth Century*. Cambridge: MIT, 1995.

Knoll Group. *75 Years of Bauhaus Design 1919-1994*. New York: Knoll Group, 1994.

_____. *Knoll Studio*. price list. New York: Knoll Group, 1995.

Kovel, Ralph & Terry, "Best Buy — Furniture Made in the Fifties." *Kovels on Antiques and Collectibles* (April 1988); "Best Seats in the House," (May 1994); "Timely Collection," (March 1996).

Larrabee, Eric & Massimo Vignelli. *Knoll Design*. New York: Harry N. Abrams, 1981.

Lightolier. *Lightolier: the first 75 years*. Jersey City: Lightolier, 1979.

Mang, Karl. *History of Modern Furniture*. New York: Harry N. Abrams, 1978.

Meadmore, Clement. *The Modern Chair: Classics in Production*. New York: Van Nostrand Reinhold, 1975.

Miller, Philip. of Howard Miller Clock Co., interview in Grandville, Michigan, June 1994.

Museum of Modern Art. *Ludwig Mies van der Rohe Furniture and Furniture Designs*. New York: Museum of Modern Art, 1977.

Nelson, George. *Chairs*. New York: Whitney, 1953; reprinted New York: Acanthus, 1994.

_____. *Display*. New York: Whitney, 1953.

_____. *Storage*. New York: Whitney, 1954.

_____. *Problems of Design*. New York: Whitney, 1957.

_____. *George Nelson on Design*. New York: Whitney Library of Design, 1979.

Neuhart, John, Marilyn Neuhart, & Ray Eames. *Eames Design*. New York: Harry N. Abrams, 1991.

Noyes, Eliot N. *Organic Design in Home Furnishings*. catalog. New York: Museum of Modern Art, 1941.

Ostergard, Derek E. *Bent Wood and Metal Furniture 1850-1946*. New York: American Federation of Arts, 1987.

_____. *George Nakashima: Full Circle*. New York: Weidenfeld & Nicolson, 1989.

Ostergard, Derek and David Hanks. "Gilbert Rohde and the Evolution of Modern Design 1927-1941." *Arts Magazine* (Oct. 1981).

Payton, Leland & Crystal. *Turned On: Decorative Lamps of the 'Fifties*. New York: Abbeville, 1989.

Pearce, Christopher. *Fifties Source Book: A Visual Guide to the Style of a Decade*. Secaucus, New Jersey: Chartwell, 1990.

Perrault, Suzanne. *Enginering & Artistry: the Tiles of Harris G. Strong*. exhibition catalog. Lambertville, New Jersey: David Rago Gallery, 1995.

Pile, John. *The Dictionary of 20th-Century Design*. New York: De Capo, 1994; originally published New York: Facts on File, 1990.

Piña, Leslie. *Designed & Signed by Georges Briard, Sascha B., Bellaire, Higgins...* Atglen, Pennsylvania: Schiffer, 1996.

Pulos, Arthur J. *The American Design Adventure*. Cambridge: MIT Press, 1988.

"Reproducing Classic Pieces." *New York Times*. (Jan. 6, 1994).

Rouland, Steve & Roger Rouland. *Heywood-Wakefield Modern Furniture*. Paducah, Kentucky: Collector Books, 1995.

Saarinen, Eero and Aline B. Saarinen. *Eero Saarinen on His Work*. New Haven: Yale U. Press, 1962.

Santini, Pier Carlo. *The Years of Italian Design: A Portrait of Cesare Cassina*. Milan: Electa, 1981.

Schildt, Göran. *Alvar Aalto: the Decisive Years*. New York: Rizzoli, 1986.

Sembach, Klaus-Jürgen, et al. *Twentieth-Century Furniture Design*. Köln, Germany: Taschen, nd.

Skinner, Inc. Fine Arts. auction catalogs. *Arts & Crafts, Art Deco & Modernism, Art Glass & Lamps*. Bolton, Oct 9, 1992; Bolton, Jan. 2, 1993; Bolton, May 22, 1993; Boston, Oct. 15 & 16; 1993; Boston, May 21, 1994; Boston, Oct. 22, 1994; Boston, Jan. 21, 1995.

Smith, C. Ray. "Edward Wormley." *Interior Design*. (June 1987).

Smithsonian Institution. *A Modern Consciousness: J. D. DePree, Florence Knoll*. exhibition catalog. Washington D. C.: Smithsonian Institution Press, 1975.

Society of Industrial Designers. *Industrial Design in America, 1954*. New York: Farrar, Straus, & Young, 1954.

Sotheby's, New York. auction catalog. *20th Century Decorative Arts*. June 10 & 11, 1993.

Sparke, Penny. *Furniture: Twentieth-Century Design*. New York: E. P. Dutton, 1986.

_____. *Italian Design 1870 to the Present*. London: Thames and Hudson, 1988.

Steelcase, Inc. *Steelcase: The First 75 Years*. Grand Rapid: Steelcase, Inc. 1987.

Steinberg, Sheila, and Kate Dooner. *Fabulous Fifties: Designs for Modern Living*. Atglen, Pennsylvania: Schiffer, 1993.

Stimpson, Miriam. *Modern Furniture Classics*. New York: Whitney Library of Design, 1987.

Treadway Gallery. auction catalogs. *20th Century Sale*. Nov. 15, 1992; Feb. 14, 1993; May 15, 1994; Oct. 23, 1994; Feb. 12, 1995; May 21, 1995; March 3, 1996.

United States Patent Office. Drawings of design patents.

Whitney Museum of Art. *High Styles: Twentieth-Century American Design*. New York: Whitney Museum, 1985.

Wilk, Christopher. *Marcel Breuer: Furniture and Interiors*. New York: Museum of Modern Art, 1981.

Zahle, Erik, ed. *A Treasury of Scandinavian Design*. New York: Golden Press, 1961.

Index